FARRAR
STRAUS
GIROUX

MARTINE FRANCK

Yves Bonnefoy
THE CURVED PLANKS

YVES BONNEFOY has published seven major poetry collections, numerous studies of literature and art, and an extensive dictionary of mythology. His work has been translated into many languages, and he is a celebrated translator of Shakespeare and Yeats. He lives in Paris.

HOYT ROGERS translates poetry and other literary works from the French, German, and Spanish. He is also the author of a book of poems, *Witnesses*, and a volume of criticism, *The Poetics of Inconstancy*. He lives in the Dominican Republic.

THE
CURVED
PLANKS

THE
CURVED
PLANKS

Yves Bonnefoy

Translated from the French
and with an afterword by Hoyt Rogers

Foreword by Richard Howard

FARRAR, STRAUS AND GIROUX

NEW YORK

Farrar, Straus and Giroux
18 West 18th Street, New York 10011

Printed in the United States of America
Originally published in 2001 by Mercure de France,
Paris, France, as *Les planches courbes*
Published in the United States in 2006 by Farrar, Straus and Giroux
First paperback edition, 2007

The Library of Congress has cataloged the hardcover edition as follows:
Bonnefoy, Yves.
    [Les planches courbes. English and French]
    The curved planks / Yves Bonnefoy ; translated by Hoyt Rogers—
1st American ed.
        p.   cm.
    English and French.
    Includes bibliographical references.
    ISBN-13: 978-0-374-18494-0 (alk. paper)

    I. Howard, Richard.   II. Title.

PQ2603.O533P53513 2006
841'.914—dc22

                                                            2005054158

Paperback ISBN-13: 978-0-374-53075-4

Designed by Cassandra J. Pappas

www.fsgbooks.com

Contents

DANS LE LEURRE DES MOTS
IN THE LURE OF WORDS

LA MAISON NATALE
THE HOUSE WHERE I WAS BORN

Acknowledgments

I would like to thank John Naughton, Mary Ann Caws, Terence Cave, Véronique Prystasz, Anne Davenport, Siri Hustvedt, Paul Auster, Nicholas Callaway, Aoibheann Sweeney, Robert Weil, Niké d'Astorg, Friedhelm Kemp, Amy Daunis Bernstein, and Peter Bernstein for their generous encouragement of this project. Lucy Vines, John Taylor, and Alastair Reid read the manuscript with care, offering valuable suggestions; and with his customary kindness, Richard Howard provided the foreword. Above all, I am grateful to Yves Bonnefoy himself, who sent me many of these poems over the years even before they were published in France, and who patiently assisted me with points of interpretation and turns of phrase.

A number of the translations in this volume, as well as portions of the afterword and translator's note, first appeared in *Poetry*, *The Harvard Review*, *Partisan Review*, *Nimrod*, the *Cumberland Poetry Review*, *AGNI*, *Notes from Europe*, *Poetry New York*, *Tin House*, and *The New Arcadia Review*. I must also acknowledge the cooperation of Mercure de France, which published the French original of the work. Finally, like so many before me, I owe a lasting debt of thanks to Jonathan Galassi of Farrar, Straus and Giroux, whose editorial discernment brought this book to fruition. His talented collaborators Susan Mitchell, Dean Nicastro, Annie Wedekind, and Jenna Dolan ably assisted him in the task.

The translation and final essays are dedicated to Eleanor, in memoriam: "Be ye doers of the word."

Foreword

The Encircling Curvature

by Richard Howard

The voluminous quantity and what it is merely civil to call the *variety* of translations into English of the poetry and even the prose of this protean French master (the most magisterial, indeed, to loom up among transatlantic *strangers* to our literature since the death of Paul Valéry), afford a proper clue to his continuously *useful* presence solicited in our contemporary literary consciousness. (As for Yves Bonnefoy's usefulness to his own compatriots, I need merely point to his translations of Shakespeare, plays and poems both: the first French versions consistenty responsible to the poetic—the ultimately *Shakespearean*—qualities of the original.)

Hoyt Rogers, as the afterword and notes to his lucid and responsible translations of Bonnefoy's late work reveal, has mastered the grand cumulus of ulterior translation, criticism, commentary, and biographical circumstance which so formidably confronts, and possibly daunts, the interpreter as well as the common reader, so that indeed *The Curved Planks* is for seasoned practitioners of this master not only a sort of precocious capstone of the still-rising edifice of the Great Work—to which common reader I cannot forbear additionally commending the magnificent study of the early baroque art, *Rome, 1630*, written thirty-five years ago and still untranslated into English—but for newcomers to Bonnefoy an excellent, even an ideal, entrance to this writer's vast creation.

For me, a fellow poet, a fellow translator, and an intense lover of Bonnefoy's *oeuvre*, it remains only to suggest a sort of embracing figure for the poems, all the poems to have appeared as I have read them over the decades, an *apparition* indeed which might stand, or sway, as a deliberately alluring general identification. That figure is a myth of recovery which will suffice, dismembered perhaps but still to be discerned in the lineaments of the Greek gods and heroes (always the first, for a French poet, to be remembered); discerned in fragments, but ultimately recognizable, actually imperative. In Bonnefoy's earlier volumes, it was the figure of Helen, but now it is Ceres, the bereft mother seeking her lost daughter at every door, who marks and monumentalizes these poems, she who gathers up the broken parts and pieces, unnamable at first and eventually recognizable as the new growth, the new year, the new hope. What was wrecked and seemingly ruined may be here discerned as a model for the poet: the goddess of earth, the "cereal mother" *in the young wheat's flame* whom Bonnefoy misses, as one misses an appointment or opportunity, yet perceives and pursues:

> Ceres, all sweat and dust,
> Who kept searching
> Throughout the earth,
> Should have waited for him.
>
> He would have granted her
> Refuge, rest,
> And what she lost
> She would have recognized . . .

          Instead, she still
          Stops, at night
          Under rustling trees,
          And knocks at closed doors.

It is the task of the poet, in our moment when so much is taken away,
to recover the myth, to reconfigure by mere words the Being that used
to inhabit the mind of the occident without a need for voiced articula-
tion, existing merely—merely!—as a presence, an aura, what George
Herbert would call "something understood." And so Bonnefoy de-
scribes the immense labor of the negative, the painful articulation of
erasure which has become necessary to the poet's calling:

          The books: he tore them all apart.
          The devastated page. Yet the light
        On the page, the increase of light. He knew
        He was becoming the blank page again.

        He went out. Torn, the visage of the world
      Took on another beauty, seemed more human now.
        In shadow play, the sky's hand reached for his.
        The stone where you see his weathered name
              Was opening, forming a word.

And then—then!—comes that "opening," that "word." One of the new
philosophers, or at least new students of the destructive verge on which
this French poet and some others live to achieve their myth ("all I have
is a voice," Auden would say), remarks about music what for me quite
as much applies or extends to poetry: it is an act of appeal, a supplica-
tion to a figure of the Other to respond not as the symbolic Other
(beloved, King, God . . .) but in the reality of its being, breaking its
own rules by showing mercy, conferring a contingent love . . . Poetry

then would have classically been an attempt to provoke *an answer* from reality: to enjoin the Other to that miracle whereby the Other offers us a look, a hand, a word . . . Perhaps it is the scar of our modernity to designate the moment when poetry *renounces* the endeavor to provoke the Other to respond. That is how I read the poet Bonnefoy at eighty:

> The planks at the prow of the boat—curved
> So the mind will have a shape to bear the brunt
> Of the unthinkable, of the unknown—are coming loose . . .
> O poetry,
> I cannot keep myself from naming you
> By name, a name no longer loved by those
> Who wander nowadays, among the ruins of speech . . .
> Your boat glides on, always dark,
> But with shadows gathered at the prow . . .
> If anything remains
> Besides the wind, the sea, the reef,
> I know that even at night you still will be
> The anchor dropped, the footsteps stumbling in the sand,
> The branches stacked, the spark
> Under sodden wood—and then, in the anxious wait
> For a wavering flame,
> The first word that ends the drawn-out silence,
> The first fire kindled in a lifeless world.

The poet reaches the visitable myth—as Henry James used to refer to the possibility in America of a *visitable past*—by proclaiming the ruin of all myth, the dissolution of any coherent story, the triumph of forgetting if it were not for the elements—stone, stones, wind, branches, the gathering wave and the collapsing surf, out of which the story begins, out of which Bonnefoy pieces together the story, the movement of a *barque*, a boat on the the dark water, the curved planks of the . . . *Argo*, was it? One governing circumstance in all this "modern" promulgation of ruin, of deperition and dissolution, is the consciousness his readers must come to that Bonnefoy is not a poet of natural objects but of natural energies—of wind and waters, of falling rock and burning wood, and that he focuses less on the necessity of things seen than upon the power of things felt. At times he is like Swinburne, nearly a blind poet, all tongue and ear and touch. His verse moves away from the art of painting (that is where his prose works its way in) toward a condition of music—we retain from Bonnefoy's lines not an image but a tonality and a rhythm:

> I knew the only task I would have
> Was to remember. And laughing,
> Bending over in the mud, I gathered up
> An armful of branches and leaves . . .
> What should I do with this wood,
> Where so much absence
> Still rang with color's sound?
>
>
> Now I understand: it was Ceres
> Who sought shelter on the night
> Someone was knocking at the door.
> Outside her beauty suddenly flared—
> Her light and her desire too, her need
>
> . . .
> We must pity Ceres, not mock her—and so
> Must meet at crossroads in deepest night,
> Call out athwart words, even with no reply:
> And make our voice, no matter how obscure,
> Love Ceres at last, who suffers and seeks.

As Lévi-Strauss tells us, even the ruin of myth is part of the myth—the modern part. The poems of *The Curved Planks* are a luxuriant recovery of fragments, a tracing of shape by the outline of its absence: a mourning that is an exultation. And the poet *looks at us with the awkwardness / Of mind when it takes up again, / Within the enigma, its task of light.*

I see that I may have been mistaken, after all, to suggest that Bonnefoy is a stranger to our American poetry, late or early, that we have no voices akin to this "calling out" of Bonnefoy's; for all the otherness of accent in these elemental, fragmented odes of the French poet, can we not hear the marveling syllables of Stevens:

> Go on, high ship, since now, upon the shore,
> The snake has left its skin upon the floor.
> Key West sank downward under massive clouds
> And silvers and greens spread over the sea. The moon
> Is at the mast-head and the past is dead.
> Her mind will never speak to me again . . .

and behind them, *beyond the genius of the sea*, the great sobbing respiration of Whitman himself on the empty shoals of Paumonok:

> O who is that ghost? that form in the dark, with tears?
> What shapeless lump is that, bent, crouch'd there on the sand?
> O storm, embodied, rising, careering with swift steps
> along the beach! . . .
> O shade so sedate and decorous by day, with calm
> countenance and regulated pace,
> But away at night as you fly, none looking—O then
> the unloosen'd ocean,
> Of tears! tears! tears!

How gratifying, then, how almost inevitable to add this new old French voice to those energies of our most powerful American masters, like them asking what destruction we are blessed by, to what rebirth we are doomed.

LES
PLANCHES
COURBES

THE
CURVED
PLANKS

LA PLUIE
D'ÉTÉ

SUMMER
RAIN

La pluie d'été

Summer Rain

LES RAINETTES, LE SOIR

I

Rauques étaient les voix
Des rainettes le soir,
Là où l'eau du bassin, coulant sans bruit,
Brillait dans l'herbe.

Et rouge était le ciel
Dans les verres vides,
Tout un fleuve la lune
Sur la table terrestre.

Prenaient ou non nos mains,
La même abondance.
Ouverts ou clos nos yeux,
La même lumière.

II

Ils s'attardaient, le soir,
Sur la terrasse
D'où partaient les chemins, de sable clair,
Du ciel sans nombre.

Et si nue devant eux
Était l'étoile,
Si proche était ce sein
Du besoin des lèvres

TREE FROGS, AT EVENING

I

At evening, the tree frogs
Sounded hoarse, where water
Trickled soundless from the basin,
Glistening in the grass.

And the sky glowed red
In the empty glasses;
A whole river of moon
Flooded the table of earth.

Our hands full or not:
The same abundance.
Our eyes open or shut:
The same light.

II

They lingered, at evening,
On the terrace where the paths
Fanned out, the shining sand
Of the numberless sky.

And the star before them
Was so naked,
This breast so close
To avid lips,

Qu'ils se persuadaient
Que mourir est simple,
Branche écartée pour l'or
De la figue mûre.

They convinced themselves
Dying is simple,
A branch pulled back
For the ripe fruit's gold.

UNE PIERRE

Matins que nous avions,
Je retirais les cendres, j'allais emplir
Le broc, je le posais sur le dallage,
Avec lui ruisselait dans toute la salle
L'odeur impénétrable de la menthe.

Ô souvenir,
Tes arbres sont en fleurs devant le ciel,
On peut croire qu'il neige,
Mais la foudre s'éloigne sur le chemin,
Le vent du soir répand son trop de graines.

A STONE

Those mornings of ours,
I would sweep up the ashes; I would fill
The jug and set it on the flagstones,
So the whole room was awash
With the fathomless smell of mint.

O memory,
Your trees blossom against the sky:
We could almost believe that it's snowing.
But thunder retreats down the path.
The evening wind sheds its excess seeds.

UNE PIERRE

Tout était pauvre, nu, transfigurable,
Nos meubles étaient simples comme des pierres,
Nous aimions que la fente dans le mur
Fût cet épi dont essaimaient des mondes.

Nuées, ce soir,
Les mêmes que toujours, comme la soif,
La même étoffe rouge, dégrafée.
Imagine, passant,
Nos recommencements, nos hâtes, nos confiances.

A STONE

Spare, bare, transfigurable: the things
In our rooms were simple as stones.
We loved the crevice in the wall, a bursting
Ear of grain that spilled out worlds.

Clouds, this evening,
The same as always, like thirst,
The same red dress, unfastened.
Imagine, passerby,
Our new beginnings, our eagerness, our trust.

LA PLUIE D'ÉTÉ

I

Mais le plus cher mais non
Le moins cruel
De tous nos souvenirs, la pluie d'été
Soudaine, brève.

Nous allions, et c'était
Dans un autre monde,
Nos bouches s'enivraient
De l'odeur de l'herbe.

Terre,
L'étoffe de la pluie se plaquait sur toi.
C'était comme le sein
Qu'eût rêvé un peintre.

II

Et tôt après le ciel
Nous consentait
Cet or que l'alchimie
Aura tant cherché.

Nous le touchions, brillant,
Sur les branches basses,
Nous en aimions le goût
D'eau, sur nos lèvres.

SUMMER RAIN

I

Yet the dearest
Of all our memories,
But not the least cruel: summer rain,
Sudden, brief.

We were walking,
Walking in another world,
Our mouths besotted
With the smell of grass.

Earth,
The cloth of the rain clung to you.
You were the breast
A painter might have dreamed.

II

And soon after, the sky
Would finally grant us
That gold the alchemists
Had so keenly sought.

We would touch its gleam
On the lower branches,
And love its taste
Of water on our lips.

Et quand nous ramassions
Branches et feuilles chues,
Cette fumée le soir puis, brusque, ce feu,
C'était l'or encore.

And when we gathered
Branches and fallen leaves,
This smoke and this sudden fire
At night were gold again.

UNE PIERRE

Une hâte mystérieuse nous appelait.
Nous sommes entrés, nous avons ouvert
Les volets, nous avons reconnu la table, l'âtre,
Le lit ; l'étoile grandissait à la croisée,
Nous entendions la voix qui veut que l'on aime
Au plus haut de l'été
Comme jouent les dauphins dans leur eau sans rive.

Dormons, ne nous sachant. Sein contre sein,
Souffles mêlés, main dans la main sans rêves.

A STONE

A mysterious haste urged us on.
We went in, we opened
The shutters, we recognized the table, the hearth,
The bed; the star was growing larger in the window,
We heard the voice that wants us to love
At summer's crest
Like dolphins playing in their sea without a shore.

Unknowing, let us sleep. Chest against chest,
Our breathing mingled, hand in hand without dreams.

UNE PIERRE

Nous nous étions fait don de l'innocence,
Elle a brûlé longtemps de rien que nos deux corps,
Et nos pas allaient nus dans l'herbe sans mémoire,
Nous étions l'illusion qu'on nomme souvenir.

Le feu naissant de soi, pourquoi vouloir
En rassembler les cendres désunies.
Au jour dit nous avons rendu ce que nous fûmes
À la flamme plus vaste du ciel du soir.

A STONE

We granted each other the gift of innocence:
For years just our two bodies fed its flames.
Our steps wandered bare through trackless grass.
We were the illusion known as memory.

Since fire's born of fire, why should we desire
To gather up its scattered ash.
On the appointed day we surrendered what we were
To a vaster blaze, the evening sky.

LES CHEMINS

I

Chemins, ô beaux enfants
Qui venaient vers nous,
L'un riant, les pieds nus
Dans les feuilles sèches.

Nous aimions sa façon
D'être en retard
Mais comme c'est permis
Quand le temps cesse,

Heureux d'entendre au loin
Sa syrinx simple
Vaincre, Marsyas enfant, le dieu
De rien que le nombre.

II

Et vite il nous menait
Là où la nuit tombe,
Lui à deux pas devant
Nous, et se retournant,

Riant toujours, prenant
À des branches, faisant
Lumière de ces fruits
De menue présence.

THE PATHS

Paths, O beautiful children
Who would come toward us—
One of them laughing, barefoot
In the dry leaves.

We loved his way
Of being late,
But as it's permitted
When time stands still,

Happy to hear his simple
Syrinx from afar:
The child Marsyas, defeating
The god of mere numbers.

II

And quickly he would lead us
Where night falls,
Two steps ahead of us
And looking back,

Still laughing, catching
At branches, making
These fruits of weightless
Presence into light.

Il allait, où n'est plus
Rien que l'on sache, mais,
Éprise de son chant, dansante, illuminée,
L'accompagnant l'abeille.

III

Cérès aurait bien dû,
Suante, empoussiérée,
L'attendre, qui cherchait
Par toute la terre.

Elle eût reçu de lui
Repos, refuge,
Et ce qu'elle perdit,
Elle l'eût reconnu

Dans son demi-jour clair
Et, d'un cri, embrassé
Et riante emporté
Dans ses mains véhémentes,

Au lieu qu'encor, de nuit
Sous des arbres bruyants
Elle s'arrête, frappe
À des portes closes.

He was going where there's nothing
We can know, yet the dazzled bee
Danced along with him,
Enamored of his song.

III

Ceres, all sweat and dust,
Who kept searching
Throughout the earth,
Should have waited for him.

He would have granted her
Refuge, rest,
And what she lost
She would have recognized

In his bright penumbra—
Embraced it with a cry
And laughing, borne it away
In her vehement hands.

Instead, she still
Stops, at night
Under rustling trees,
And knocks at closed doors.

HIER, L'INACHEVABLE

Notre vie, ces chemins
Qui nous appellent
Dans la fraîcheur des prés
Où de l'eau brille.

Nous en voyons errer
Au faîte des arbres
Comme cherche le rêve, dans nos sommeils,
Son autre terre.

Ils vont, leurs mains sont pleines
D'une poussière d'or,
Ils entrouvrent leurs mains
Et la nuit tombe.

YESTERDAY, WITHOUT END

Our life, these paths
That call us
In the coolness of meadows
Where water shines.

Some of them go roaming
On the crowns of trees,
Just as in our sleep, a dream
Will seek its other earth.

They wander, hands full
Of golden dust.
They spread their fingers,
And night falls.

UNE PIERRE

Nos ombres devant nous, sur le chemin,
Avaient couleur, par la grâce de l'herbe,
Elles eurent rebond, contre des pierres.

Et des ombres d'oiseaux les effleuraient
En criant, ou bien s'attardaient, là où nos fronts
Se penchaient l'un vers l'autre, se touchant presque
Du fait de mots que nous voulions nous dire.

A STONE

The grass granted color to our shadows,
Before us on the path; and once
They rebounded on some stones.

Bird-shadows, too, brushed by them
With a cry, or lingered where our foreheads
Leaned together so we almost touched
Because of words we wanted to share.

UNE PIERRE

Plus de chemins pour nous, rien que l'herbe haute,
Plus de passage à gué, rien que la boue,
Plus de lit préparé, rien que l'étreinte
À travers nous des ombres et des pierres.

Mais claire cette nuit
Comme nous désirions que fût notre mort.
Elle blanchit les arbres, ils s'élargissent.
Leur feuillage : du sable, puis de l'écume.
Même au-delà du temps le jour se lève.

A STONE

No more paths for us, nothing but unscythed grass.
No more ford to cross, nothing but mud.
No more bed laid out, nothing but stones
And shadows embracing through us.

Still this night is bright,
As we desired our death might be.
It whitens the trees, they expand.
Their foliage: sand, then foam.
Day is breaking, even beyond time.

QUE CE MONDE DEMEURE !

I

Je redresse une branche
Qui s'est rompue. Les feuilles
Sont lourdes d'eau et d'ombre
Comme ce ciel, d'encore

Avant le jour. Ô terre,
Signes désaccordés, chemins épars,
Mais beauté, absolue beauté,
Beauté de fleuve,

Que ce monde demeure,
Malgré la mort !
Serrée contre la branche
L'olive grise.

II

Que ce monde demeure,
Que la feuille parfaite
Ourle à jamais dans l'arbre
L'imminence du fruit !

Que les huppes, le ciel
S'ouvrant, à l'aube,
S'envolent à jamais, de dessous le toit
De la grange vide,

LET THIS WORLD ENDURE

I

I right a broken branch.
The leaves are heavy
With water and shadow
Like this sky now, before

The dawn of day. O earth,
Clashing signs, scattered paths,
But beauty, beauty absolute,
The beauty of a river:

Let this world endure,
In spite of death.
The gray olive
Clings to the branch.

II

Let this world endure,
Let the perfect leaf
Halo forever
The ripening fruit.

Let the hoopoes, when the sky
Opens at dawn,
Fly forever from under the roof
Of the empty barn,

Puis se posent, là-bas
Dans la légende,
Et tout est immobile
Une heure encore.

III

Que ce monde demeure !
Que l'absence, le mot
Ne soient qu'un, à jamais,
Dans la chose simple.

L'un à l'autre ce qu'est
La couleur à l'ombre,
L'or du fruit mûr à l'or
De la feuille sèche.

Et ne se dissociant
Qu'avec la mort
Comme brillance et eau quittent la main
Où fond la neige.

IV

Oh, que tant d'évidence
Ne cesse pas
Comme s'éteint le ciel
Dans la flaque sèche,

Then alight over there
In legend;
And all is motionless
An hour more.

III

Let this world endure,
Let absence and word
Fuse forever
In simple things.

Let word be to absence
As color is to shadow,
Gold of ripe fruit
To gold of dry leaves:

Not parting until death,
Like a snowflake on a hand—
The water vanishes,
So does the gleam.

IV

Let so pure a presence
Never cease
Like sky that fades
From water as it dries.

Que ce monde demeure
Tel que ce soir,
Que d'autres que nous prennent
Au fruit sans fin,

Que ce monde demeure,
Qu'entre, à jamais,
La poussière brillante du soir d'été
Dans la salle vide,

Et ruisselle à jamais
Sur le chemin
L'eau d'une heure de pluie
Dans la lumière.

v

Que ce monde demeure,
Que les mots ne soient pas
Un jour ces ossements
Gris, qu'auront becquetés,

Criant, se disputant,
Se dispersant,
Les oiseaux, notre nuit
Dans la lumière.

Let this world remain
As it is tonight:
Let others, beyond ourselves,
Partake of the endless fruit.

Let this world endure,
Let the shining dust of summer eve
Forever enter
The empty room,

And the water of an hour's rain
Stream forever
In the light
Along the path.

v

Let this world endure,
And words not be one day
These graying bones
That birds will peck,

Screeching, squabbling,
Wheeling apart,
Birds that are our night
Within the light.

Que ce monde demeure
Comme cesse le temps
Quand on lave la plaie
De l'enfant qui pleure.

Et lorsque l'on revient
Dans la chambre sombre
On voit qu'il dort en paix,
Nuit, mais lumière.

VI

Bois, disait celle qui
S'était penchée,
Quand il pleurait, confiant,
Après sa chute.

Bois, et qu'ouvre ta main
Ma robe rouge,
Que consente ta bouche
À sa bonne fièvre.

De ton mal presque plus
Rien ne te brûle,
Bois de cette eau, qui est
L'esprit qui rêve.

Let this world endure
Just as time stands still
While we clean the cut
Of a weeping child.

And then returning
To the darkened room,
We see he sleeps in peace:
Night that is light.

VI

Drink, she said,
Bending over him,
As he wept full of trust
After his fall.

Drink, and let your hand
Open my red dress,
Your mouth consent
To its good fever.

The hurt that burned you
Has almost drained away.
Drink of this water, which is
The mind that dreams.

VII

Terre, qui vint à nous
Les yeux fermés
Comme pour demander
Qu'une main la guide.

Elle dirait : nos voix
Qui se prennent au rien
L'une de l'autre soient
Notre suffisance.

Nos corps tentent le gué
D'un temps plus large,
Nos mains ne sachent rien
De l'autre rive.

L'enfant naisse du rien
Du haut du fleuve
Et passe, dans le rien,
De barque en barque.

VIII

Et encore : l'été
N'aura qu'une heure
Mais la nôtre soit vaste
Comme le fleuve.

VII

Earth, who came to us
Eyes closed
As though to ask
For a guiding hand.

She would say: Let our voices,
Drawn to the nothing
In each other, be
All that we need.

Let our bodies try
To ford a wider time,
Our hands not know
The other shore.

Upstream, let the child be born
From nothing, and pass
Downstream in nothing
From boat to boat.

VIII

And again: summer will last
No more than an hour.
But let our hour be
Vast as the river.

Car c'est dans le désir
Et non le temps
Qu'a puissance l'oubli
Et que mort travaille,

Et vois, mon sein est nu
Dans la lumière
Dont les peintures sombres, indéchiffrées,
Passent rapides.

Forgetfulness has power
And death does its work
Only in desire,
Not in time.

See, my breast is naked
In the light, whose somber
Paintings, undeciphered,
Quickly flicker by.

UNE VOIX

I

Tout cela, mon ami,
Vivre, qui noue
Hier, notre illusion,
À demain, nos ombres.

Tout cela, et qui fut
Si nôtre, mais
N'est que ce creux des mains
Où eau ne reste.

Tout cela ? Et le plus
Notre bonheur :
L'envol lourd de la huppe
Au creux des pierres.

II

Et puisse être le ciel
Notre façon d'être,
Avec ombre et couleurs
Qui se déchirent

Mais dans la hâte même
De la nuée
Ont visage d'enfant
Qui vient de naître,

A VOICE

All that, my friend,
Is how we live, tying
Yesterday, our illusion,
To tomorrow, our shades.

All that, once so much ours,
And now no more
Than this hollow of our hands
Where no water remains.

All that? And most of all
Our happiness:
The hoopoe's heavy flight
In the hollow of the rocks.

II

The sky's way of being
Should be ours,
With shadows and colors
That disperse

But in the cloud's very haste
Wear the face
Of a child just born.

Foudre qui dort encore,
Les traits en paix,
Souriante comme avant
Qu'il y ait langage.

Lightning that still sleeps,
The features at peace,
Smiling the smile before
The dawn of words.

UNE PIERRE

Ils ont vécu au temps où les mots furent pauvres,
Le sens ne vibrait plus dans les rythmes défaits,
La fumée foisonnait, enveloppant la flamme,
Ils craignaient que la joie ne les surprendrait plus.

Ils ont dormi. Ce fut par détresse du monde.
Passaient dans leur sommeil des souvenirs
Comme des barques dans la brume, qui accroissent
Leurs feux, avant de prendre le haut du fleuve.

Ils se sont éveillés. Mais l'herbe est déjà noire.
Les ombres soient leur pain et le vent leur eau.
Le silence, l'inconnaissance leur anneau,
Une brassée de nuit tout leur feu sur terre.

A STONE

They lived in the time when words were poor.
In rhythms undone, meaning pulsed no more.
Smoke billowed up and shrouded the flame.
They feared that joy would not surprise them again.

They slept and slept, by the world distressed.
Memories passed through their sleep
Like boats in the fog, stoking their fires
Before they head upstream.

They woke. But the grass had already turned black.
Let wind be their water, and shadow their bread,
Unknowing and silence their ring.
An armful of night all their fire on earth.

Je déplace du pied
Entre d'autres pierres
Cette large, qui couvre
Des vies, peut-être.

Et c'est vrai : de nombreuses
Sont là, qui courent
De toutes parts, aveugles
Par soudain trop de jour.

Mais vite les voici
Rédimées par l'herbe.
Je n'ai troublé qu'un peu
La vie sans mémoire.

Comme il fait beau, ce soir !
À peine si
Je sais, sur ce chemin,
Que j'existe encore.

"AMONG OTHER STONES . . ."

Among other stones
I dislodge with my foot
This large one that covers
Other lives, perhaps.

And true enough: many
Are there, milling
Helter-skelter, blinded
By sudden light.

But there they go, quickly
Redeemed by the grass.
I've scarcely disturbed
Unremembering life.

How beautiful the sky is,
This evening . . . I hardly
Know, on this path,
If I still exist.

Un même effacement,
Désirer, prendre,
Presque de même poids
Être, ne pas être.

Et aller, ce chemin
Ou bien cet autre,
Ainsi sans hâte va, s'évaporant,
La pluie dans l'herbe.

Odeurs, couleurs, saveurs,
Le même songe,
Colombes dans l'ailleurs
Du roucoulement.

"THE SAME EFFACEMENT . . ."

The same effacement
In wanting or taking;
In being or not being,
About the same weight.

And this path
Or the other: we go
Like the rain, when it mists
Unhurried in the grass.

Smells, colors, tastes,
All the same dream:
Doves in the elsewhere
Of their cooing.

UNE PIERRE

Il se souvient
De quand deux mains terrestres attiraient
Sa tête, la pressaient
Sur des genoux de chaleur éternelle.

Étale le désir ces jours, parmi ses rêves,
Silencieux le peu de houle de sa vie,
Les doigts illuminés gardaient clos ses yeux.

Mais le soleil du soir, la barque des morts,
Touchait la vitre, et demandait rivage.

A STONE

He remembers
When two earthly hands
Held his head
On knees of eternal warmth.

These days of becalmed desire, among his dreams,
The mild sea-swell of his life all silent,
Glowing fingers kept his eyes shut.

But the evening sun, the skiff of the dead,
Was touching the window, asking for berth.

UNE PIERRE

Les livres, ce qu'il déchira,
La page dévastée, mais la lumière
Sur la page, l'accroissement de la lumière,
Il comprit qu'il redevenait la page blanche.

Il sortit. La figure du monde, déchirée,
Lui parut d'une beauté autre, plus humaine.
La main du ciel cherchait sa main dans le jeu des ombres,
La pierre, où vous voyez que son nom s'efface,
S'entrouvrait, se faisait une parole.

A STONE

The books: he tore them all apart.
The devastated page. Yet the light
On the page, the increase of light. He knew
He was becoming the blank page again.

He went out. Torn, the visage of the world
Took on another beauty, seemed more human now.
In shadow play, the sky's hand reached for his.
The stone where you see his weathered name
Was opening, forming a word.

Passant, ce sont des mots. Mais plutôt que lire
Je veux que tu écoutes : cette frêle
Voix comme en ont les lettres que l'herbe mange.

Prête l'oreille, entends d'abord l'heureuse abeille
Butiner dans nos noms presque effacés.
Elle erre de l'un à l'autre des deux feuillages,
Portant le bruit des ramures réelles
À celles qui ajourent l'or invisible.

Puis sache un bruit plus faible encore, et que ce soit
Le murmure sans fin de toutes nos ombres.
Il monte, celui-ci, de sous les pierres
Pour ne faire qu'une chaleur avec l'aveugle
Lumière que tu es encore, ayant regard.

Simple te soit l'écoute ! Le silence
Est un seuil où, par voie de ce rameau
Qui casse imperceptiblement sous ta main qui cherche
À dégager un nom sur une pierre,

Nos noms absents désenchevêtrent tes alarmes,
Et pour toi qui t'éloignes, pensivement,
Ici devient là-bas sans cesser d'être.

"PASSERBY, THESE ARE WORDS . . ."

Passerby, these are words. But instead of reading
I want you to listen: to this frail
Voice like that of letters eaten by grass.

Lend an ear, hear first of all the happy bee
Foraging in our almost rubbed-out names.
It flits between two sprays of leaves,
Carrying the sound of branches that are real
To those that filigree the unseen gold.

Then know an even fainter sound, and let it be
The endless murmuring of all our shades.
Their whisper rises from beneath the stones
To fuse into a single heat with that blind
Light you are as yet, who can still gaze.

Listen simply, if you will. Silence is a threshold
Where, unfelt, a twig breaks in your hand
As you try to disengage
A name upon a stone:

And so our absent names untangle your alarms.
And for you who move away, pensively,
Here becomes there without ceasing to be.

Sur la pierre tachée
De mousses l'ombre
Bouge. On dirait de nymphes
Dansant ensemble.

Et qu'un peu de soleil
Passe, leur chevelure
Brille, ainsi ferait l'or
Dans le vase sombre.

La vie s'achèvera,
La vie demeure.
De même joue l'enfant
Parmi trop de rêves.

"On the moss-stained . . ."

On the moss-stained
Rock the shadows
Move. Almost like nymphs
In their dance.

When a sliver of sun
Shines through, their hair
Glints as gold might do
In a somber crucible.

Life will end.
Life endures.
The same as a child, playing
With too many dreams.

La pluie sur le ravin

Rain Falls on the Ravine

I

Il pleut, sur le ravin, sur le monde. Les huppes
Se sont posées sur notre grange, cimes
De colonnes errantes de fumée.
Aube, consens à nous aujourd'hui encore.

De la première guêpe
J'ai entendu l'éveil, déjà, dans la tiédeur
De la brume qui ferme le chemin
Où quelques flaques brillent. Dans sa paix
Elle cherche, invisible. Je pourrais croire
Que je suis là, que je l'écoute. Mais son bruit
Ne s'accroît qu'en image. Mais sous mes pas
Le chemin n'est plus le chemin, rien que mon rêve
De la guêpe, des huppes, de la brume.

J'aimais sortir à l'aube. Le temps dormait
Dans les braises, le front contre la cendre.
Dans la chambre d'en haut respiraient en paix
Nos corps que découvrait la décrue des ombres.

I

Rain falls on the ravine, on the world.
Hoopoes alighting on our barn
Crown wandering columns of smoke.
Dawn, consent to us once more today.

I hear the first wasp
Already rousing in the warmth
Of the fog that seals this path
Where a few puddles shine. The wasp searches
In peace, invisible. I could believe
That I am here, that I listen; but its hum
Deepens only in my mind. The path
Beneath my feet is no longer the path,
Only my dream
Of the wasp, the hoopoes, the fog.

I liked setting out at dawn. Time lay asleep
In the embers, forehead pressed against the ashes.
In the room upstairs the shadows' ebb
Uncovered our bodies, breathing in peace.

II

Pluie des matins d'été, inoubliable
Clapotement comme d'un premier froid
Sur la vitre du rêve ; et le dormeur
Se déprenait de soi et demandait
À mains nues dans ce bruit de la pluie sur le monde
L'autre corps, qui dormait encore, et sa chaleur.

(Bruit de l'eau sur le toit de tuiles, par rafales,
Avancée de la chambre par à-coups
Dans la houle, qui s'enfle, de la lumière.
L'orage
A envahi le ciel, l'éclair
S'est fait d'un grand cri bref,
Et les richesses de la foudre se répandent.)

III

Je me lève, je vois
Que notre barque a tourné, cette nuit.
Le feu est presque éteint.
Le froid pousse le ciel d'un coup de rame.

II

Rain of summer mornings, plashing
Unforgettably, like a first chill
On the windowpane of dream.
The sleeper, parting from himself
In this rain that pelted the world,
Asked with naked hands for the other body,
Still asleep, and for its heat.

(Squalls slap the roof tiles,
The room thrusts ahead by fits and starts
In the surging swell of light.
The storm
Has invaded the sky, lightning
Cracks with a loud shout
And the riches of the thunderbolt pour out.)

III

I get up and see that our boat
Has veered in the night.
The fire has died down.
The chill pushes the sky with a flick of its oar.

Et la surface de l'eau n'est que lumière,
Mais au-dessous ? Troncs d'arbres sans couleur, rameaux
Enchevêtrés comme le rêve, pierres
Dont le courant rapide a clos les yeux
Et qui sourient dans l'étreinte du sable.

The water's surface is light alone.
But underneath? Faded tree-trunks,
Boughs entangled like a dream, stones
With eyes the rapid stream has closed
And that smile in the sand's embrace.

À même rive

Toward the Same Shore

I

Parfois prend le miroir
Entre ciel et chambre
Dans ses mains le minime
Soleil terrestre.

Et des choses, des noms
C'est comme si
Les voies, les espérances se rejoignaient
À même rive.

On se prend à rêver
Que les mots ne sont pas
À l'aval de ce fleuve, fleuve de paix,
Trop pour le monde,

Et que parler n'est pas
Trancher l'artère
De l'agneau qui, confiant,
Suit la parole.

I

Between sky and room
Sometimes our mirror
Takes the small earthly
Sun in its hands,

As though
The paths, the hopes
Of things and names
Joined on the same shore.

We start to dream
That downstream from this river
Of peace, words will not ask
Too much of the world,

That words will not cut
The throat of the lamb
That trustfully
Follows our speech.

II

Rêver : que la beauté
Soit vérité, la même
Évidence, un enfant
Qui avance, étonné, sous une treille.

Il se dresse et, heureux
De tant de lumière,
Tend sa main pour saisir
La grappe rouge.

III

Et plus tard on l'entend
Seul dans sa voix
Comme s'il allait nu
Sur une plage

Et tenait un miroir
Où tout du ciel
Trouerait, à grands rayons, recolorerait
Tout de la terre.

Il s'arrête pourtant
Ici ou là,
Son pied pousse, distrait,
L'eau dans le sable.

II

Dreaming that beauty
Is truth, their radiance
One and the same: a child
Awed by the grapevine
Over the door.

Standing tall, happy
With so much light,
He reaches up to grasp
That cluster of red fruit.

III

And later you hear him,
Alone in his voice,
As though he strolled
Naked on a beach

Holding a mirror
Where piercing rays
From the limitless sky
Color earth anew.

Still he stops
Here and there, distractedly,
His foot nudging water
Into the sand.

LA VOIX
LOINTAINE

THE FARAWAY
VOICE

I

Je l'écoutais, puis j'ai craint de ne plus
L'entendre, qui me parle ou qui se parle.
Voix lointaine, un enfant qui joue sur la route,
Mais la nuit est tombée, quelqu'un appelle

Là où la lampe brille, où la porte grince
En s'ouvrant davantage ; et ce rayon
Recolore le sable où dansait une ombre,
Rentre, chuchote-t-on, rentre, il est tard.

(Rentre, a-t-on chuchoté, et je n'ai su
Qui appelait ainsi, du fond des âges,
Quelle marâtre, sans mémoire ni visage,
Quel mal souffert avant même de naître.)

II

Ou bien je l'entendais dans une autre salle.
Je ne savais rien d'elle sinon l'enfance.
Des années ont passé, c'est presque une vie
Qu'aura duré ce chant, mon bien unique.

Elle chantait, si c'est chanter, mais non,
C'était plutôt entre voix et langage
Une façon de laisser la parole
Errer, comme à l'avant incertain de soi,

I listened, then feared I no longer
Heard it, speaking to me or itself.
A faraway voice, a child plays on the road.
But night has fallen, and someone calls

Where the lamp shines, where the door
Creaks open; and that ray of light
Gilds the sand again, where a shadow danced.
Come home, someone whispers. Come home, it's late.

(Come home, someone whispered. I couldn't tell
Who was calling like this from the depths of time:
What evil woman there, without memory or face;
What ill the child had suffered, before she was born.)

II

Or else I was hearing her in another room.
All I knew of her was her childhood.
Years have passed, and this song
Has lasted almost a lifetime, all that I own.

She sang, if it was singing. No,
It hovered between singing and speech:
A way of letting her words
Wander uncertainly, groping ahead.

Et parfois ce n'étaient pas même des mots,
Rien que le son dont des mots veulent naître
Le son d'autant d'ombre que de lumière,
Ni déjà la musique ni plus le bruit.

III

Et je l'aimais comme j'aime ce son
Au creux duquel rajeunirait le monde,
Ce son qui réunit quand les mots divisent,
Ce beau commencement quand tout finit.

Syllabe brève puis syllabe longue,
Hésitation de l'iambe, qui voudrait
Franchir le pas du souffle qui espère
Et accéder à ce qui signifie.

Telle cette lumière dans l'esprit
Qui brille quand on quitte, de nuit, sa chambre,
Une lampe cachée contre son coeur,
Pour retrouver une autre ombre dansante.

IV

Et la vie a passé, mais te garda
Vive mon illusion, de ces mains savantes
Qui trient parmi les souvenirs, qui en recousent
Presque invisiblement les déchirures.

At times there were not even words, only
Sound they hoped would give them birth.
Sound as much of shadow as of light—
Not yet music, but no longer simply sound.

III

I loved her voice as I love that sound
Whose depths rejuvenate the world.
The sound that reunites when words divide,
The beautiful rebirth when all else ends.

Two syllables, a short and then a long:
The iamb hesitates, but also yearns
To leap beyond the breath that merely hopes
And enter into all that meaning gives.

It is the light that glimmers in the mind
When in the night we rise and leave our room,
A lamp clutched tight against our heart, to find
Another shadow, dancing in its glow.

IV

So life has passed—though my old illusion
Kept the voice alive. How skillfully its hands
Sort through reminiscences, mending
Almost seamlessly all that has been torn.

Sauf : que faire de ce lambeau d'étoffe rouge ?
On le trouve dans sa mémoire quand on déplace
Les années, les images ; et, brusques, des larmes
Montent, et l'on se tait dans ses mots d'autrefois.

Parler, presque chanter, avoir rêvé
De plus même que la musique, puis se taire
Comme l'enfant qu'envahit le chagrin
Et qui se mord la lèvre, et se détourne.

v

Elle chantait, mais comme se parlant :
Qui a tiré sa barque sur la rive,
Qui a posé sa rame sur le sable,
Qui est passé, que nous ne savons pas ?

Qui d'un pied nu aura laissé l'empreinte,
Qui a rendu iridescente l'eau,
Qui préserva la braise sous la cendre,
Qui dessina ce visage d'enfant ?

C'était un chant de rien que quelques notes,
Qui a voulu le chant dans la parole ?
— Nul n'a voulu, nul n'est venu ni parle,
Nul n'est passé, que nous ne sûmes pas.

All except this: a scrap of red cloth.
Sifting through the years, the images,
We find it in our memory. Then tears
Well up, our silence at bygone words.

To speak, almost to sing; to have dreamed
Of even more than music . . . Then silence,
Like a child assailed by grief
Who bites his lip, and turns away.

v

She sang, as though speaking to herself:
Who dragged his boat onto the bank,
Who laid his oar out on the sand,
Who passed by, without our knowing?

Who left his footprint on the ground,
Who changed water into light,
Who saved these embers in the ash,
Who drew childhood's face?

The song had just a few notes.
Who wanted speech to sing?
—No one. No one came, no one speaks,
No one passed by, or we would have known.

VI

Et nul n'a bu au verre que je pose
Ni pris du fruit qui était devant moi,
Un peu de vent fait remuer la poussière
D'herbes sèches, de graines, sur le chemin.

L'été : un éblouissement comme est la neige,
Celle que vient légère et ne dure pas,
Et rien de nous n'en trouble la lumière
D'eau qui s'est condensée puis s'évapore.

D'où la sérénité, même l'allégresse
De ces instants qui savent que n'est rien.
Flocon la main qui avait pris le verre,
Autres flocons l'été, le ciel, les souvenirs.

VII

Ne cesse pas, voix dansante, parole
De toujours murmurée, âme des mots
Qui et colore et dissipe les choses
Les soirs d'été où il n'est plus de nuit.

Voix qui porte de l'être dans l'apparence,
Qui les mêle comme flocons de même neige,
Voix qui presque s'est tue, lorsque le rêve
Demanda trop et crut presque obtenir.

VI

And no one drank from the glass I raised
Nor ate of the fruit in front of me;
A puff of wind stirs up the dust
Of dry grass and seeds along the path.

Summer dazzles like a lightly
Drifting snow that will not last.
Nothing of ourselves beclouds the glow
Of snowflakes melting back to air.

There is serenity and even joy
When instants know that nothing is.
Snow the hand that raised the glass, snow
The summer and the sky. Snow our memories.

VII

Never cease, dancing voice, speech
That murmurs through all time, soul of words
That colors things and makes them disappear
On summer nights, when night forgets to fall.

Voice that grants being to appearance,
Blending them like flakes in the selfsame snow.
Voice that almost ended when our dream
Asked too much, and thought it was bestowed.

Et qui jouera à clore nos paupières
En se pressant riante contre nous,
Puis nous verrons ces signes sur le sable
Qu'égratigna en dansant son pied nu.

VIII

Ne cesse pas, voix proche, il fait jour encore,
Si belle est même la lumière, comme jamais.
Reviens dehors, petite vie dansante. Si le désir
De danser, même seule, t'enveloppe,

Vois, tu as sur le sable assez de lumière
Pour jouer avec l'ombre de ton corps.
Et même, sans plus craindre, offrir tes mains
Au rire qui s'enténèbre dans les arbres.

Ô musique, ô rumeur de tant d'autres mondes,
N'est-ce pas là ce que tu désirais
Le soir qu'Amour te fit, comme il fut dit,
Le coeur serré dans la salle descendre ?

IX

Elle chantait : « Je suis, je ne suis pas,
Je tiens la main d'une autre que je suis,
Je danse parmi mes ombres, l'une se tourne
Vers moi, elle est riante, elle est sans visage.

Voice that plays at covering our eyes,
Brushing up against us with a laugh;
Then we find these marks along the sand,
Traced by her bare, dancing feet.

VIII

Never cease, nearby voice. On and on
Day is deepening the beauty of the light.
Dancer, little spirit, come back out. If the wish
To dance enfolds you, even all alone,

See? On the sand there's light enough
For you and your shadow to play.
Fearless at last, you can reach out your hands
To the laughter that darkens in the trees.

O music, distant hum of other worlds,
Was this not what you desired, on that evening
When (the poet says), Love made you descend
Into the room, with torment in your heart?

IX

She sang: "I am and I am not.
I hold the hand of another that I am.
As I dance among my shadows, one
Wheels merrily, to face me with no face.

Je danse avec mes ombres sur le chemin,
Je ne trouve qu'en elles ma joie d'être,
Je sais pourtant qu'avant l'aube le fer
Déchirera l'étoffe de la danse.

Et je me tourne alors vers cette plus gauche,
Cette plus hésitante et comme étonnée
Qui se tient en retrait, dans la musique :
Vois, ce n'est que pour toi que je ris et danse. »

X

Et ombre elle était bien, une fantasque
Découpe du langage sur le ciel,
Ainsi nuées et arbres quand ils mêlent
Leurs fumées dans l'eau calme, et c'est le soir.

Ombre mais le seul bien qui soit au monde
Puisqu'elle puise à toute chose simple
L'eau qui déborde, avec l'odeur des feuilles,
Du broc posé sur les dalles sonores.

XI

Elle chantait, et j'ai eu dans ses mots
De quoi presque finir ma longue guerre.
Quand je venais près d'elle, je touchais
Ses mains, je regardais ses doigts défaire

I dance with my shadows on the path;
My joy in life I find in them alone.
And still I know that long before the dawn
A sword will rend the weaving of this dance.

And then I turn to a more awkward shade
Who wavers and seems stunned, outside
The music's shifting ring. 'You see,'
I say. 'It's all for you I laugh and dance.'"

X

Shadow she was, a whimsical
Outline of words against the sky,
As clouds and trees mingle their mist
On waters calmed, when evening starts to fall.

Just a shade, yet the world's only good,
Since she draws from every simple thing
The water that spills with an odor of leaves
When our jug makes the flagstones ring.

XI

She sang, and her words were like a gift
That almost let me end my endless war.
As I drew nearer to her now and touched
Her hands, I saw her fingers loose the thread

Ce fil qui a ses nœuds dans l'invisible.
Était-elle dehors à jouer, une simple
Servante enfant qui a charge du monde ?
Était-elle la Parque, qui aurait moins

À mettre à mort qu'à mener sous des arbres
Où, souriante à qui serait près d'elle :
« Écoute, dirait-elle, les mots se taisent,
Leur son n'est plus qu'un bruit, et le bruit cesse » ?

That ties its knots in the invisible.
Was that child, playing outside, a simple
Servant girl in charge of the world?
The Fate who would not have to kill,

But only lead us under the trees; and say,
Smiling at the one who happens to be near:
"Listen, the words fall silent. Their song
Is only sound, and now the sound will end."

DANS LE LEURRE DES MOTS

IN THE LURE
OF WORDS

I

C'est le sommeil d'été cette année encore,
L'or que nous demandons, du fond de nos voix,
À la transmutation des métaux du rêve.
La grappe des montagnes, des choses proches,
A mûri, elle est presque le vin, la terre
Est le sein nu où notre vie repose
Et des souffles nous environnent, nous accueillent.
Telle la nuit d'été, qui n'a pas de rives,
De branche en branche passe le feu léger.
Mon amie, c'est là nouveau ciel, nouvelle terre,
Une fumée rencontre une fumée
Au-dessus de la disjonction des deux bras du fleuve.

Et le rossignol chante une fois encore
Avant que notre rêve ne nous prenne,
Il a chanté quand s'endormait Ulysse
Dans l'île où faisait halte son errance,
Et l'arrivant aussi consentit au rêve,
Ce fut comme un frisson de sa mémoire
Par tout son bras d'existence sur terre
Qu'il avait replié sous sa tête lasse.
Je pense qu'il respira d'un souffle égal
Sur la couche de son plaisir puis du repos,
Mais Vénus dans le ciel, la première étoile,
Tournait déjà sa proue, bien qu'hésitante,
Vers le haut de la mer, sous des nuées,

I

Again this year, at our voices' core,
Summer sleep is the gold we ask
From our dreams' transmuted ore.
Mountains cluster like grapes, and things nearby
Have also ripened, almost into wine. Our life
Reposes on the naked breast of earth,
And breezes surround us with their welcome.
This is the summer night without a shore.
Weightless fire spills from branch to branch.
My friend, here are new heaven and new earth.
Above the river's parted arms
Two hazes merge in a single mist.

Once more the nightingale sings
Before our dream overtakes us.
So it sang as Ulysses fell asleep
On the isle where his wandering paused.
He too consented to that dream,
Like a shudder of his memory
Along the arm
Of his whole life on earth,
Folded underneath his weary head.
I think he breathed an equal breath
On the couch of pleasure as of rest.
But in the sky Venus, first of all the stars,
Already turned a wavering prow
Toward open seas—and then began to drift

Puis dérivait, barque dont le rameur
Eût oublié, les yeux à d'autres lumières,
De replonger sa rame dans la nuit.

Et par la grâce de ce songe que vit-il ?
Fut-ce la ligne basse d'un rivage
Où seraient claires des ombres, claire leur nuit
À cause d'autres feux que ceux qui brûlent
Dans les brumes de nos demandes, successives
Pendant notre avancée dans le sommeil ?
Nous sommes des navires lourds de nous-mêmes,
Débordants de choses fermées, nous regardons
À la proue de notre périple toute une eau noire
S'ouvrir presque et se refuser, à jamais sans rive.
Lui cependant, dans les plis du chant triste
Du rossignol de l'île de hasard,
Pensait déjà à reprendre sa rame
Un soir, quand blanchirait à nouveau l'écume,
Pour oublier peut-être toutes les îles
Sur une mer où grandit une étoile.

Aller ainsi, avec le même orient
Au-delà des images qui chacune
Nous laissent à la fièvre de désirer,
Aller confiants, nous perdre, nous reconnaître
À travers la beauté des souvenirs
Et le mensonge des souvenirs, à travers l'affre
De quelques-uns, mais aussi le bonheur

Below the clouds, a boat whose rower
Had forgotten, looking for other lights,
To dip his oar again into the night.

And thanks to this dream, what did he see?
Was it the low outline of a coast
Where shadows gleamed, their night
Aglow with other fires than those that burn
In the fog of our demands, unfurling
Bank on bank as we voyage into sleep?
Ships weighed down by ourselves, we burst
With locked-up things. From our journey's prow
We peer as blackened waters almost open up for us
And then refuse, perpetually without a shore.
But he, even as the nightingale enfolded him
In mournful song on that island of chance,
Already pondered taking up his oar again
Some evening when the foam whitened anew.
Perhaps he would forget all islands then,
And sail a sea whose star forever grows.

To go like this, with the same guiding star,
Beyond the images that all, unfailingly,
Leave us to the fever of desiring—
To go in trust, to stray, to recognize ourselves
Through the beauty, and also the illusion,
Of our memories . . . the pain of some, yet
The happiness of others, those whose fire

D'autres, dont le feu court dans le passé en cendres,
Nuée rouge debout au brisant des plages,
Ou délice des fruits que l'on n'a plus.
Aller, par au-delà presque le langage,
Avec rien qu'un peu de lumière, est-ce possible
Ou n'est-ce pas que l'illusoire encore,
Dont nous redessinons sous d'autres traits
Mais irisés du même éclat trompeur
La forme dans les ombres qui se resserrent ?
Partout en nous rien que l'humble mensonge
Des mots qui offrent plus que ce qui est,
Ou disent autre chose que ce qui est,
Les soirs non tant de la beauté qui tarde
À quitter une terre qu'elle a aimée,
La façonnant de ses mains de lumière,
Que de la masse d'eau qui de nuit en nuit
Dévale avec grand bruit dans notre avenir.

Nous mettons nos pieds nus dans l'eau du rêve,
Elle est tiède, on ne sait si c'est de l'éveil
Ou si la foudre lente et calme du sommeil
Trace déjà ses signes dans des branches
Qu'une inquiétude agite, puis c'est trop sombres
Pour qu'on y reconnaisse des figures
Que ces arbres s'écartent, devant nos pas.
Nous avançons, l'eau monte à nos chevilles,
Ô rêve de la nuit, prends celui du jour
Dans tes deux mains aimantes, tourne vers toi

Still flickers through the ashes of the past:
The tall red cloud above the breaking surf,
Or our delight in fruits we no longer have.
To go, almost beyond our words,
With nothing but a feeble glow—
Could that be possible? Or is it sham again,
A few altered strokes sketching out a form
That glitters in the serried dark
With the old deceptive gleam?
And nothing in us anywhere but humble lies,
Words that offer more than what there is
Or utter something else than what there is.
Evenings—not of beauty that prolongs
Its slow farewells to an earth that it has loved,
Still molding it with hands of light—
But sheets of water tumbling down
That roar through our future, night after night.

We dip our bare feet in the water of dream:
How warm it is . . . We cannot tell if we still wake
Or if the calm, unhurried thunderbolt of sleep
Is tracing signs already in the boughs.
Disquiet stirs the leaves: these trees
That part before our steps are too obscure
For us to recognize the figures there.
We move on. The water rises to our ankles.
O dream of night, hold the dream of day
In your loving hands. Tilt that face toward yours.

Son front, ses yeux, obtiens avec douceur
Que son regard se fonde au tien, plus sage,
Pour un savoir que ne déchire plus
La querelle du monde et de l'espérance,
Et qu'unité prenne et garde la vie
Dans la quiétude de l'écume, où se reflète,
Soit beauté, à nouveau, soit vérité, les mêmes
Étoiles qui s'accroissent dans le sommeil.

Beauté, suffisante beauté, beauté ultime
Des étoiles sans signifiance, sans mouvement.
À la poupe est le nautonier, plus grand que le monde,
Plus noir, mais d'une matité phosphorescente.
Le léger bruit de l'eau à peine troublée,
C'est, bientôt, le silence. Et on ne sait encore
Si c'est rive nouvelle, ou le même monde
Que dans les plis fiévreux du lit terrestre,
Ce sable qu'on entend qui crisse sous la proue.
On ne sait si on touche à une autre terre,
On ne sait si des mains ne se tendent pas
Du sein de l'inconnu accueillant pour prendre
La corde que nous jetons, de notre nuit.

Et demain, à l'éveil,
Peut-être que nos vies seront plus confiantes
Où des voix et des ombres s'attarderont,
Mais détournées, calmes, inattentives,
Sans guerre, sans reproche, cependant

Drink gently from those eyes until their gaze
Merges with your wiser watchfulness.
Instill a knowledge that our world's dispute
With hope can no longer undermine.
Let unity preserve and shelter life
In the quietude of foam, where truth
Is mirrored, beauty reflected anew:
The same two stars sleep magnifies.

Beauty, beauty sufficient, ultimate beauty
Of the stars, meaningless and motionless.
Larger and darker than the world, the ferryman
Stands at the stern, black but phosphorescent.
A faint plash barely mars the water:
Soon it lapses into silence. Hearing the sand
That crunches under our prow, we do not know
If we have reached another shore, or still remain
In the fevered folds of our earthly bed. We do not know
If we make landfall in another world; we do not know
If hands reach out from that welcoming unknown
To take the rope we toss them from our night.

Tomorrow when we wake,
Perhaps our lives will be more trusting:
Voices and shadows will still tarry there,
But they will turn away from us,
Tranquil and unconcerned,
Without reproaches, without war.

Que l'enfant près de nous, sur le chemin,
Secouera en riant sa tête immense,
Nous regardant avec la gaucherie
De l'esprit qui reprend à son origine
Sa tâche de lumière dans l'énigme.

Il sait encore rire,
Il a pris dans le ciel une grappe trop lourde,
Nous le voyons l'emporter dans la nuit.
Le vendangeur, celui qui peut-être cueille
D'autres grappes là-haut dans l'avenir,
Le regarde passer, bien que sans visage.
Confions-le à la bienveillance du soir d'été,
Endormons-nous . . .

                    . . . La voix que j'écoute se perd,
Le bruit de fond qui est dans la nuit la recouvre.
Les planches de l'avant de la barque, courbées
Pour donner forme à l'esprit sous le poids
De l'inconnu, de l'impensable, se desserrent.
Que me disent ces craquements, qui désagrègent
Les pensées ajointées par l'espérance ?
Mais le sommeil se fait indifférence.
Ses lumières, ses ombres : plus rien qu'une
Vague qui se rabat sur le désir.

And all the while, laughingly, that child beside us
On the path will shake his limitless head.
He looks at us with the awkwardness
Of mind when it takes up again,
Within the enigma, its task of light.

He still knows how to laugh.
The bunch of grapes he plucked from the sky
Weighs too much. We see him bear it off into the night.
Faceless, the harvester who will be culling
Other grapes up there, perhaps,
In future times, watches him go by.
Let's entrust the child to summer evening's kindness,
And fall asleep . . .

            . . . The voice I heard trails off,
Submerged at last in the humming of the night.
The planks at the prow of the boat—curved
So the mind will have a shape to bear the brunt
Of the unthinkable, of the unknown—are coming loose.
What do these creaks and splinters tell me now,
Sundering the thoughts that hope had joined?
But sleep resolves into indifference.
Its shadows and lights: no more than a
Wave curling back on desire.

II

Et je pourrais
Tout à l'heure, au sursaut du réveil brusque,
Dire ou tenter de dire le tumulte
Des griffes et des rires qui se heurtent
Avec l'avidité sans joie des vies primaires
Au rebord disloqué de la parole.
Je pourrais m'écrier que partout sur terre
Injustice et malheur ravagent le sens
Que l'esprit a rêvé de donner au monde,
En somme, me souvenir de ce qui est,
N'être que la lucidité qui désespère
Et, bien que soit retorse
Aux branches du jardin d'Armide la chimère
Qui leurre autant la raison que le rêve,
Abandonner les mots à qui rature,
Prose, par évidence de la matière,
L'offre de la beauté dans la vérité,

Mais il me semble aussi que n'est réelle
Que la voix qui espère, serait-elle
Inconsciente des lois qui la dénient.
Réel, seul, le frémissement de la main qui touche
La promesse d'une autre, réelles, seules,
Ces barrières qu'on pousse dans la pénombre,
Le soir venant, d'un chemin de retour.

11

And presently,
Waking with a start,
I could say or try to say the tumult,
The clash of claws and jeers,
The greed of joyless beasts
At the disjointed edge of speech.
I could exclaim that everywhere
Injustice and misfortune have defaced
The meaning mind has dreamed
Of giving to the world; or in a word,
I could recall what is, I could become
No more than open-eyed despair.
In the garden of Armida, the chimera
Among the boughs is shrewd enough
To hoodwink reason as well as dream:
And so I could abandon words
To those who cross them out—
Whose prose, in the presence
Of matter, crosses out the offer
Beauty makes to truth.

But it also seems to me that only the voice
That hopes is real, even when unconscious
Of the laws that would belie it. Only the hand
That trembles is real, touching the promise
Of someone else's hand. Only these gates
We push are real, going home at dusk

Je sais tout ce qu'il faut rayer du livre,
Un mot pourtant reste à brûler mes lèvres.

Ô poésie,
Je ne puis m'empêcher de te nommer
Par ton nom que l'on n'aime plus parmi ceux qui errent
Aujourd'hui dans les ruines de la parole.
Je prends le risque de m'adresser à toi, directement,
Comme dans l'éloquence des époques
Où l'on plaçait, la veille des jours de fête,
Au plus haut des colonnes des grandes salles,
Des guirlandes de feuilles et de fruits.

Je le fais, confiant que la mémoire,
Enseignant ses mots simples à ceux qui cherchent
À faire être le sens malgré l'énigme,
Leur fera déchiffrer, sur ses grandes pages,
Ton nom un et multiple, où brûleront
En silence, un feu clair,
Les sarments de leurs doutes et de leurs peurs.
« Regardez, dira-t-elle, dans le seul livre
Qui s'écrive à travers les siècles, voyez croître
Les signes dans les images. Et les montagnes
Bleuir au loin, pour vous être une terre.
Écoutez la musique qui élucide
De sa flûte savante au faîte des choses
Le son de la couleur dans ce qui est. »

In the penumbra of our path. I know
All the things I should strike from the book,
And yet a word remains, burning my lips.

O poetry,
I cannot keep myself from naming you
By name, a name no longer loved by those
Who wander nowadays, among the ruins of speech.
I take the risk, I address you face to face
As in the eloquence of former times,
When on the eve of celebrations
Garlands of leaves and fruit
Were hung on the columns of great rooms.

I name you now, confident that memory
Will teach its simple words to those who seek
To make meaning be, despite the enigma;
That on its ample pages it will trace
Your single, multiple name; that there, silently,
The vine-shoots of their doubts and fears
Will be consumed in a lucid flame.
"Read," says memory, "the only book
Written through the centuries, and see
The signs that grow among the images.
For you the mountains' distant blue
Becomes an earth. At the summit of the real,
Hear how music plays its knowing flute,
Lighting the sounds of color in all that is."

Ô poésie,
Je sais qu'on te méprise et te dénie,
Qu'on t'estime un théâtre, voire un mensonge,
Qu'on t'accable des fautes du langage,
Qu'on dit mauvaise l'eau que tu apportes
À ceux qui tout de même désirent boire
Et déçus se détournent, vers la mort.

Et c'est vrai que la nuit enfle les mots,
Des vents tournent leurs pages, des feux rabattent
Leurs bêtes effrayées jusque sous nos pas.
Avons-nous cru que nous mènerait loin
Le chemin qui se perd dans l'évidence,
Non, les images se heurtent à l'eau qui monte,
Leur syntaxe est incohérence, de la cendre,
Et bientôt même il n'y a plus d'images,
Plus de livre, plus de grand corps chaleureux du monde
À étreindre des bras de notre désir.

Mais je sais tout autant qu'il n'est d'autre étoile
À bouger, mystérieusement, auguralement,
Dans le ciel illusoire des astres fixes,
Que ta barque toujours obscure, mais où des ombres
Se groupent à l'avant, et même chantent
Comme autrefois les arrivants, quand grandissait
Devant eux, à la fin du long voyage,
La terre dans l'écume, et brillait le phare.

O poetry,
I know you are scoffed at and denied,
Dismissed as theater, and even as a lie,
Reviled for the wrongs of language.
They call the water brackish that you bring
To those who still aspire to drink,
And who turn disappointed toward death.

And it is true that words are swollen with night,
That winds turn their pages and fires flush
Their startled beasts, almost under our feet.
Did we believe the path that fades away
Into the obvious would lead us far?
No: the images collide as flooding mounts,
Their syntax lapses, incoherent, turns to ash.
And soon no images survive—no book,
No great warm body of the world
We can embrace with the arms of our desire.

And yet I also know no other star
That moves, auguring a mystery,
Through the sky's illusion of fixed orbs:
Your boat glides on, always dark,
But with shadows gathered at the prow.
They sing like settlers of former times,
When at the end of a lengthy voyage
Earth waxed larger in the foam,
And a beacon shone.

Et si demeure
Autre chose qu'un vent, un récif, une mer,
Je sais que tu seras, même de nuit,
L'ancre jetée, les pas titubants sur le sable,
Et le bois qu'on rassemble, et l'étincelle
Sous les branches mouillées, et, dans l'inquiète
Attente de la flamme qui hésite,
La première parole après le long silence,
Le premier feu à prendre au bas du monde mort.

If anything remains
Besides the wind, the sea, the reef,
I know that even at night you still will be
The anchor dropped, the footsteps stumbling in the sand,
The branches stacked, the spark
Under sodden wood—and then, in the anxious wait
For a wavering flame,
The first word that ends the drawn-out silence,
The first fire kindled in a lifeless world.

LA MAISON
NATALE

THE HOUSE WHERE
I WAS BORN

I

Je m'éveillai, c'était la maison natale,
L'écume s'abattait sur le rocher,
Pas un oiseau, le vent seul à ouvrir et fermer la vague,
L'odeur de l'horizon de toutes parts,
Cendre, comme si les collines cachaient un feu
Qui ailleurs consumait un univers.
Je passai dans la véranda, la table était mise,
L'eau frappait les pieds de la table, le buffet.
Il fallait qu'elle entrât pourtant, la sans-visage
Que je savais qui secouait la porte
Du couloir, du côté de l'escalier sombre, mais en vain,
Si haute était déjà l'eau dans la salle.
Je tournais la poignée, qui résistait,
J'entendais presque les rumeurs de l'autre rive,
Ces rires des enfants dans l'herbe haute,
Ces jeux des autres, à jamais les autres, dans leur joie.

II

Je m'éveillai, c'était la maison natale.
Il pleuvait doucement dans toutes les salles,
J'allais d'une à une autre, regardant
L'eau qui étincelait sur les miroirs
Amoncelés partout, certains brisés ou même
Poussés entre des meubles et les murs.
C'était de ces reflets que, parfois, un visage
Se dégageait, riant, d'une douceur

I

I woke: the house where I was born.
Spume battered the rock. Not a bird;
Only wind, closing and opening the wave.
The horizon all around smelled of ash,
As though somewhere beyond the hills
A fire were devouring a universe. I went
Into the sideroom: the table had been set.
Water struck the sideboard, the table legs.
Yet she had to come in, the faceless one;
I knew she was rattling the hallway door,
There near the darkened stairs. But in vain:
Water was already flooding the room.
I turned the knob; the door wouldn't give.
I almost heard them on that far-off shore—
Children laughing in high grass. Others
Laughing, always others, in their joy.

II

I woke: the house where I was born.
Rain was falling softly in all the rooms.
I went from room to room, looking
At the water as it sparkled on the mirrors
Piled up everywhere—some shattered, others
Even tucked between the furniture and walls.
At times in those reflections I could see
A face appear, laughing with a sweetness

*

De plus et autrement que ce qu'est le monde.
Et je touchais, hésitant, dans l'image,
Les mèches désordonnées de la déesse,
Je découvrais sous le voile de l'eau
Son front triste et distrait de petite fille.
Étonnement entre être et ne pas être,
Main qui hésite à toucher la buée,
Puis j'écoutais le rire s'éloigner
Dans les couloirs de la maison déserte.
Ici rien qu'à jamais le bien du rêve,
La main tendue qui ne traverse pas
L'eau rapide, où s'efface le souvenir.

III

Je m'éveillai, c'était la maison natale,
Il faisait nuit, des arbres se pressaient
De toutes parts autour de notre porte,
J'étais seul sur le seuil dans le vent froid,
Mais non, nullement seul, car deux grands êtres
Se parlaient au-dessus de moi, à travers moi.
L'un, derrière, une vieille femme, courbe, mauvaise,
L'autre debout dehors comme une lampe,
Belle, tenant la coupe qu'on lui offrait,
Buvant avidement de toute sa soif.
Ai-je voulu me moquer, certes non,
Plutôt ai-je poussé un cri d'amour
Mais avec la bizarrerie du désespoir,

Other than the world's, beyond its ken.
And hesitant, in the image I touched
The disheveled tresses of the goddess;
Through the veil of water I beheld
Her sad, distracted brow of a little girl.
Perplexity between what is and what
Is not, hand that hesitates on misted glass . . .
Then I listened as the laughter trailed away
Down the corridors of the deserted house.
Here the only thing we ever own is dream:
Though we reach out, our hand can never cross
The rapid stream where memories recede.

III

I woke: the house where I was born.
In the night, on every side, trees
Crowded round our door. I stood there
On the threshold, alone in the freezing wind.
But no, not alone at all. Two large figures
Were speaking above me, speaking through me:
One was an old woman, evil and stooped;
The other stood outside, radiant as a lamp,
Raising the cup that had been offered her.
Eagerly she drank, with all her thirst.
Did I mean to mock her? Surely not.
The strangled sound I made was a cry of love,
But it rang with the strangeness of despair.

Et le poison fut partout dans mes membres,
Cérès moquée brisa qui l'avait aimée.
Ainsi parle aujourd'hui la vie murée dans la vie.

IV

Une autre fois.
Il faisait nuit encore. De l'eau glissait
Silencieusement sur le sol noir,
Et je savais que je n'aurais pour tâche
Que de me souvenir, et je riais,
Je me penchais, je prenais dans la boue
Une brassée de branches et de feuilles,
J'en soulevais la masse, qui ruisselait
Dans mes bras resserrés contre mon cœur.
Que faire de ce bois où de tant d'absence
Montait pourtant le bruit de la couleur,
Peu importe, j'allais en hâte, à la recherche
D'au moins quelque hangar, sous cette charge
De branches qui avaient de toute part
Des angles, des élancements, des pointes, des cris.

Et des voix, qui jetaient des ombres sur la route,
Ou m'appelaient, et je me retournais,
Le cœur précipité, sur la route vide.

And then the poison seized me, head to toe.
Mocked, Ceres doomed the one who loved her:
So says today the life that's walled inside of life.

IV

Another time.
Night again. In silence
Water slid on the darkened ground.
I knew the only task I would have
Was to remember. And laughing,
Bending over in the mud, I gathered up
An armful of branches and leaves.
I held them to my chest; they dripped
As I clutched them against my heart.
What should I do with this wood,
Where so much absence
Still rang with color's sound?
It didn't matter. I hurried on, looking
For a warehouse at least, reeling
Under branches that bristled with snags,
Throbbing hopes, points and cries.

And voices were casting their shadows
On the road, or calling me. And my heart raced
As I turned around, to face the empty road.

V

Or, dans le même rêve
Je suis couché au plus creux d'une barque,
Le front, les yeux contre ses planches courbes
Où j'écoute cogner le bas du fleuve.
Et tout d'un coup cette proue se soulève,
J'imagine que là, déjà, c'est l'estuaire,
Mais je garde mes yeux contre le bois
Qui a odeur de goudron et de colle.
Trop vastes les images, trop lumineuses,
Que j'ai accumulées dans mon sommeil,
Pourquoi revoir, dehors,
Les choses dont les mots me parlent, mais sans convaincre,
Je désire plus haute ou moins sombre rive.

Et pourtant je renonce à ce sol qui bouge
Sous le corps qui se cherche, je me lève,
Je vais dans la maison de pièce en pièce,
Il y en a maintenant d'innombrables,
J'entends crier des voix derrière des portes,
Je suis saisi par ces douleurs qui cognent
Aux chambranles qui se délabrent, je me hâte,
Trop lourde m'est la nuit qui dure, j'entre effrayé
Dans une salle encombrée de pupitres,
Vois, me dit-on, ce fut ta salle de classe,
Vois sur les murs tes premières images,
Vois, c'est l'arbre, vois, là, c'est le chien qui jappe,
Et cette carte de géographie, sur la paroi

V

In the same dream
I lie in the hollow of a hull,
Eyes and forehead pressed to the curved planks
Where I can hear the river knocking.
Then suddenly the prow rides up. Already,
I imagine, this must be the river's mouth.
Even so I wedge my eyes against the wood
That smells of pitch and glue.
The images garnered in my sleep
Have been too vast, too luminous.
Why look outside again, why see the things
Words say to me, though unconvincingly.
I desire a higher or less somber shore.

But I renounce this floor that moves
Under my uncertain body. I get up,
I walk through the house from room to room,
And now the rooms are numberless.
I hear voices shouting behind the doors.
I'm distressed by these torments that pound
At the decrepit doorjambs. I hurry by.
The night drags on. Fear weighs me down.
I enter a room crowded with desks.
Look, I'm told. This classroom was yours.
Look at the wall. Those were your first images.
Look, there's the tree, and there's the yelping dog.
And this map that yellows on the wall,

Jaune, ce décolorement des noms et des formes,
Ce dessaisissement des montagnes, des fleuves,
Par la blancheur qui transit le langage,
Vois, ce fut ton seul livre. L'Isis du plâtre
Du mur de cette salle, qui s'écaille,
N'a jamais eu, elle n'aura rien d'autre
À entrouvrir pour toi, refermer sur toi.

VI

Je m'éveillai, mais c'était en voyage,
Le train avait roulé toute la nuit,
Il allait maintenant vers de grands nuages
Debout là-bas, serrés, aube que déchirait
À des instants le lacet de la foudre.
Je regardais l'avènement du monde
Dans les buissons du remblai ; et soudain
Cet autre feu, en contrebas d'un champ
De pierres et de vignes. Le vent, la pluie
Rabattaient sa fumée contre le sol,
Mais une flamme rouge s'y redressait,
Prenant à pleines mains le bas du ciel.
Depuis quand brûlais-tu, feu des vignerons ?
Qui t'avait voulu là et pour qui sur terre ?

Après quoi il fit jour ; et le soleil
Jeta de toutes parts ses milliers de flèches

This slow discoloring of names and shapes,
These rivers, these mountains that disappear
In the whiteness invading language:
This was your only book. Isis—
The plaster wall peeling in this room—
Has never had, will never have
Anything else to open up to you
Or close to you again.

VI

I woke, but we were traveling.
The train had lumbered through the night.
Now it rolled toward massive clouds
That loomed in a cluster up ahead.
From time to time, lightning's whip tore the dawn.
I watched the advent of the world
Through the brush of the embankment; and suddenly
That other fire below, in a field
Of stones and vines. Rain and wind
Stamped its smoke down to the ground,
But the reddish flame stood up again,
Seizing the whole lower sky in its hands.
Grape-growers' fire, how long had you burned?
Who wanted you there? For whom on this earth?

Then daylight broke. The sun
Shot its thousand arrows everywhere

Dans le compartiment où des dormeurs
La tête dodelinait encore, sur la dentelle
Des coussins de lainage bleu. Je ne dormais pas,
J'avais trop l'âge encore de l'espérance,
Je dédiais mes mots aux montagnes basses
Que je voyais venir à travers les vitres.

VII

Je me souviens, c'était un matin, l'été,
La fenêtre était entrouverte, je m'approchais,
J'apercevais mon père au fond du jardin.
Il était immobile, il regardait
Où, quoi, je ne savais, au-dehors de tout,
Voûté comme il était déjà mais redressant
Son regard vers l'inaccompli ou l'impossible.
Il avait déposé la pioche, la bêche,
L'air était frais ce matin-là du monde,
Mais impénétrable est la fraîcheur même, et cruel
Le souvenir des matins de l'enfance.
Qui était-il, qui avait-il été dans la lumière,
Je ne le savais pas, je ne sais encore.

Mais je le vois aussi, sur le boulevard,
Avançant lentement, tant de fatigue
Alourdissant ses gestes d'autrefois.
Il repartait au travail, quant à moi
J'errais avec quelques-uns de ma classe

In that compartment where sleepers' heads
Still nodded, on the lace of blue wool cushions.
But I was not sleeping. I still
Lived too deep in the age of hope.
I devoted my words to low mountains
I saw coming through the windows.

VII

I remember, it was a summer morning.
The window was half open. As I came closer,
I saw my father there in the garden.
He stood motionless. Where he was looking,
Or at what, I couldn't tell—outside everything.
Stooped as he already was, he lifted his gaze
Toward the unachieved, or the impossible.
He had laid down the pickaxe, the spade.
The air was cool on that morning of the world.
But coolness is impenetrable, and cruel
Are the memories of childhood mornings.
Who he was, who he had been in the light:
I did not know, I still do not know.

But I also see him on the boulevard
Slowly walking forward, so much tiredness
Weighing down his gestures of former days.
He was going back to work. As for me,
I was strolling with some classmates

Au début de l'après-midi sans durée encore.
À ce passage-là, aperçu de loin,
Soient dédiés les mots qui ne savent dire.

(Dans la salle à manger
De l'après-midi d'un dimanche, c'est en été,
Les volets sont fermés contre la chaleur,
La table débarrassée, il a proposé
Les cartes puisqu'il n'est pas d'autres images
Dans la maison natale pour recevoir
La demande du rêve, puis il sort
Et aussitôt l'enfant maladroit prend les cartes,
Il substitue à celles de l'autre jeu
Toutes les cartes gagnantes, puis il attend
Avec fièvre, que la partie reprenne, et que celui
Qui perdait gagne, et si glorieusement
Qu'il y voie comme un signe, et de quoi nourrir
Il ne sait, lui l'enfant, quelle espérance.
Après quoi deux voies se séparent, et l'une d'elles
Se perd, et presque tout de suite, et ce sera
Tout de même l'oubli, l'oubli avide.

J'aurai barré
Cent fois ces mots partout, en vers, en prose,
Mais je ne puis
Faire qu'ils ne remontent dans ma parole.)

In the early afternoon, timeless as yet.
To his passing by, observed from afar, let me
Dedicate these words that don't know how to say.

(In the dining room
on a Sunday afternoon; it's summer.
The shutters are closed against the heat.
The table cleared, he proposes a game of cards.
In the house where I was born
There are no other images to still
The demands of dream. Later he steps out,
And the awkward child takes up the cards;
He replaces the ones that had been dealt
With a winning hand, then waits with bated breath
For the game to begin again. Now the loser would win,
So gloriously that he sees it
As something of a sign, something that might nourish—
What, being just a child, he cannot know—some kind of hope.
But after this their paths diverge. One of them
Is lost, almost right away. And forgetfulness,
Forgetfulness devours all.

I've crossed these words out everywhere
A hundred times, in verse, in prose,
But I cannot: always they well up again,
And tell their truth.)

VIII

J'ouvre les yeux, c'est bien la maison natale,
Et même celle qui fut et rien de plus.
La même petite salle à manger dont la fenêtre
Donne sur un pécher qui ne grandit pas.
Un homme et une femme se sont assis
Devant cette croisée, l'un face à l'autre,
Ils se parlent, pour une fois. L'enfant
Du fond de ce jardin les voit, les regarde.
Il sait que l'on peut naître de ces mots.
Derrière les parents la salle est sombre.
L'homme vient de rentrer du travail. La fatigue
Qui a été le seul nimbe des gestes
Qu'il fut donné à son fils d'entrevoir
Le détache déjà de cette rive.

IX

Et alors un jour vint
Où j'entendis ce vers extraordinaire de Keats,
L'évocation de Ruth « when, sick for home,
She stood in tears amid the alien corn ».

VIII

I open my eyes:
This is the house where I was born,
Surely the one that was and nothing more.
The same small dining room looks out
On a peach tree that never grows.
A man and a woman have sat down
In front of the window, face to face.
They talk to each other for once. The child
Sees them from the garden: he watches them,
Knowing that life can be born from these words.
Behind his parents the room is dark.
The man has just returned from work. Fatigue,
The only nimbus of his gestures
Ever granted his son to glimpse,
Detaches him already from this shore.

IX

Then came the day when I first heard
That extraordinary verse of Keats,
Evoking Ruth "when, sick for home,
She stood in tears amid the alien corn."

Or, de ces mots
Je n'avais pas à pénétrer le sens
Car il était en moi depuis l'enfance,
Je n'ai eu qu'à le reconnaître, et à l'aimer
Quand il est revenu du fond de ma vie.

Qu'avais-je eu, en effet, à recueillir
De l'évasive présence maternelle
Sinon le sentiment de l'exil et les larmes
Qui troublaient ce regard cherchant à voir
Dans les choses d'ici le lieu perdu ?

X

La vie, alors ; et ce fut à nouveau
Une maison natale. Autour de nous
Le grenier d'au-dessus l'église défaite,
Le jeu d'ombres léger des nuées de l'aube,
Et en nous cette odeur de la paille sèche
Restée à nous attendre, nous semblait-il,
Depuis le dernier sac monté, de blé ou seigle,
Dans l'autrefois sans fin de la lumière
Des étés tamisés par les tuiles chaudes.
Je pressentais que le jour allait poindre,
Je m'éveillais, et je me tourne encore
Vers celle qui rêva à côté de moi
Dans la maison perdue. À son silence

I did not have to grapple
With the meaning of these words,
Since it was in me from my childhood.
I only needed to recognize and love
What had returned from the depths of my life.

And truly, what could I have gleaned
From that evasive mother's presence
If not the sense of exile? Tears
Clouding her eyes that tried to see
A long-lost place in the here and now.

X

Life, then: and once again
A house where I was born. The granary
Above a ruined church enfolded us.
Pale clouds shadow-played at dawn.
It seemed this odor of dry straw
Had waited to pervade us—ever since
They stored the last sack of wheat or rye
In those unended days of bygone radiance,
Of summers filtering through sun-warmed tiles.
I sensed that dawn was going to break,
That soon I would wake up. And now I turn again
To her who dreamed beside me
In the house we have lost. This evening,

Soient dédiés, au soir,
Les mots qui semblent ne parler que d'autre chose.

(Je m'éveillais,
J'aimais ces jours que nous avions, jours préservés
Comme va lentement un fleuve, bien que déjà
Pris dans le bruit de voûtes de la mer.
Ils avançaient, avec la majesté des choses simples,
Les grandes voiles de ce qui est voulaient bien prendre
L'humaine vie précaire sur le navire
Qu'étendait la montagne autour de nous.
Ô souvenir,
Elles couvraient des claquements de leur silence
Le bruit, d'eau sur les pierres, de nos voix,
Et en avant ce serait bien la mort,
Mais de cette couleur laiteuse du bout des plages
Le soir, quand les enfants
Ont pied, loin, et rient dans l'eau calme, et jouent encore.)

XI

Et je repars, et c'est sur un chemin
Qui monte et tourne, bruyères, dunes
Au-dessus d'un bruit encore invisible, avec parfois
Le bien furtif du chardon bleu des sables.
Ici, le temps se creuse, c'est déjà
L'eau éternelle à bouger dans l'écume,
Je suis bientôt à deux pas du rivage.

To her silence, let me dedicate these words
That only seem to speak of something else.

(I was almost awake.
How I loved those days of ours, preserved
The way a river slows, already caught
In the resounding arches of the sea.
They moved with the majesty of simple things.
Vast sails, the sails of all that is, agreed to lift
Our fragile human life aboard the ship
That the mountains wrapped around us.
O memory,
Their luffing silence decked the sound
Our voices made, like water on stones.
No doubt, on the horizon would be death:
But milky as that shade where beaches end,
At evening, when the children still touch bottom
Far into the sea, laughing in tranquil waters, and still play.)

XI

And I start out again, along a path
That climbs and turns. Moors and dunes,
Above a sound as yet invisible. In the sand,
Now and then, blue thistle's furtive gift.
Time goes hollow here, becomes
Eternal water surging in the foam.
And soon I stand two steps from the sea.

Et je vois qu'un navire attend au large,
Noir, tel un candélabre à nombre de branches
Qu'enveloppent des flammes et des fumées.
Qu'allons-nous faire ? crie-t-on de toutes parts,
Ne faut-il pas aider ceux qui là-bas
Nous demandent rivage ? Oui, clame l'ombre,
Et je vois des nageurs qui, dans la nuit,
Se portent vers le navire, soutenant,
D'une main au-dessus de l'eau agitée,
Des lampes, aux longues banderoles de couleur.
La beauté même, en son lieu de naissance,
Quand elle n'est encore que vérité.

XII

Beauté et vérité, mais ces hautes vagues
Sur ces cris qui s'obstinent. Comment garder
Audible l'espérance dans le tumulte,
Comment faire pour que vieillir, ce soit renaître,
Pour que la maison s'ouvre, de l'intérieur,
Pour que ce ne soit pas que la mort qui pousse
Dehors celui qui demandait un lieu natal ?

Je comprends maintenant que ce fût Cérès
Qui me parut, de nuit, chercher refuge
Quand on frappait à la porte, et dehors,
C'était d'un coup sa beauté, sa lumière
Et son désir aussi, son besoin de boire

I discover that a ship waits offshore:
A black candelabra, all its boughs
Engulfed in flames and smoke.
What can we do? people cry out on every side.
Shouldn't we help the voyagers out there
Who're asking us for berth? Yes, darkness shouts.
And then I see how swimmers in the night
Race toward the ship with one hand raised
Above the stormy swells, holding lamps
That stream with colored pennants.
Beauty itself in its place of birth,
When not yet anything but truth.

XII

Beauty and truth. But tall waves crash
On cries that still persist. The voice of hope,
Above the din—how can we make it heard?
How can growing old become rebirth?
How can the house be opened from within,
So death will not turn out the child
Who kept asking for a native place?

Now I understand: it was Ceres
Who sought shelter on the night
Someone was knocking at the door.
Outside her beauty suddenly flared—
Her light and her desire too, her need

Avidement au bol de l'espérance
Parce qu'était perdu mais retrouvable
Peut-être, cet enfant qu'elle n'avait su,
Elle pourtant divine et riche de soi,
Soulever dans la flamme des jeunes blés
Pour qu'il ait rire, dans l'évidence qui fait vivre,
Avant la convoitise du dieu des morts.

Et pitié pour Cérès et non moquerie,
Rendez-vous à des carrefours dans la nuit profonde,
Cris d'appels au travers des mots, même sans réponse,
Parole même obscure mais qui puisse
Aimer enfin Cérès qui cherche et souffre.

To slake her thirst with the cup of hope:
She might still find that child again,
Even if lost. Though rich with herself,
Rich with her divinity, she had not known
How to lift her child in the young wheat's flame,
Laughing in the simple light that gives us life—
Before the god of the dead, and all his greed.

We must pity Ceres, not mock her—and so
Must meet at crossroads in deepest night,
Call out athwart words, even with no reply:
And make our voice, no matter how obscure,
Love Ceres at last, who suffers and seeks.

LES PLANCHES
COURBES

THE CURVED
PLANKS

L'homme était grand, très grand, qui se tenait sur la rive, près de la barque. La clarté de la lune était derrière lui, posée sur l'eau du fleuve. À un léger bruit l'enfant qui s'approchait, lui tout à fait silencieusement, comprenait que la barque bougeait, contre son appontement ou une pierre. Il tenait serrée dans sa main la petite pièce de cuivre.

« Bonjour, monsieur », dit-il d'une voix claire mais qui tremblait parce qu'il craignait d'attirer trop fort l'attention de l'homme, du géant, qui était là immobile. Mais le passeur, absent de soi comme il semblait l'être, l'avait déjà aperçu, sous les roseaux. « Bonjour, mon petit, répondit-il. Qui es-tu ?

— Oh, je ne sais pas, dit l'enfant.

— Comment, tu ne sais pas ! Est-ce que tu n'as pas de nom ? »

L'enfant essaya de comprendre ce que pouvait être un nom.

« Je ne sais pas », dit-il à nouveau, assez vite.

« Tu ne sais pas ! Mais tu sais bien ce que tu entends quand on te fait signe, quand on t'appelle ?

— On ne m'appelle pas.

— On ne t'appelle pas quand il faut rentrer à la maison ? Quand tu as joué dehors et que c'est l'heure pour ton repas, pour dormir ? N'as-tu pas un père, une mère ? Où est ta maison, dis-moi. »

Et l'enfant de se demander maintenant ce que c'est qu'un père, une mère ; ou une maison.

« Un père, dit-il, qu'est-ce que c'est ? »

Le passeur s'assit sur une pierre, près de sa barque. Sa voix vint de moins loin dans la nuit. Mais il avait eu d'abord une sorte de petit rire.

The man who stood on the bank near the boat was tall, very tall. Behind him moonlight nestled on the waters. As the boy approached the river in utter silence, he heard faint thumps: he knew the boat must be bumping gently against the dock, or a stone. He held the small copper coin clutched tight in his hand.

"Hello, sir," he said in a clear voice, though it trembled. He feared he was making himself too obtrusive to the ferryman. The giant loomed there, motionless. He seemed to be distracted; yet he'd already noticed the child, under the reeds. "Hello, my boy," he replied. "Who are you?"

"Oh, I don't know," said the child.

"What, you don't know! Don't you have a name?"

The child tried to grasp what a name might be. "I don't know," he said again, quickly enough.

"You don't know! But you have to know what you hear when somebody waves at you or calls!"

"Nobody calls me."

"Nobody calls you when it's time to come home? When you've been playing outside and it's mealtime, or bedtime? Don't you have a father, a mother? Where is your home? Tell me."

Now the boy was wondering what a father might be, or a mother, or a home.

"A father," he said. "What's that?"

The ferryman sat down on a stone near his boat. Though at first he had laughed a bit, now his voice came from less far away in the night.

« Un père ? Eh bien, celui qui te prend sur ses genoux quand tu pleures, et qui s'assied près de toi le soir lorsque tu as peur de t'endormir, pour te raconter une histoire. »

L'enfant ne répondit pas.

« Souvent on n'a pas eu de père, c'est vrai, reprit le géant comme après quelque réflexion. Mais alors il y a ces jeunes et douces femmes, dit-on, qui allument le feu, qui vous assoient près de lui, qui vous chantent une chanson. Et quand elles s'éloignent, c'est pour faire cuire des plats, on sent l'odeur de l'huile qui chauffe dans la marmite.

— Je ne me souviens pas de cela non plus », dit l'enfant de sa légère voix cristalline. Il s'était approché du passeur qui maintenant se taisait, il entendait sa respiration égale, lente. « Je dois passer le fleuve, dit-il. J'ai de quoi payer le passage. »

Le géant se pencha, le prit dans ses vastes mains, le plaça sur ses épaules, se redressa et descendit dans sa barque, qui céda un peu sous son poids. « Allons, dit-il. Tiens-toi bien fort à mon cou ! » D'une main, il retenait l'enfant par une jambe, de l'autre il planta la perche dans l'eau. L'enfant se cramponna à son cou d'un mouvement brusque, avec un soupir. Le passeur put prendre alors la perche à deux mains, il la retira de la boue, la barque quitta la rive, le bruit de l'eau s'élargit sous les reflets, dans les ombres.

Et un instant après un doigt toucha son oreille. « Écoute, dit l'enfant, veux-tu être mon père ? » Mais il s'interrompit aussitôt, la voix brisée par les larmes.

« Ton père ! Mais je ne suis que le passeur ! Je ne m'éloigne jamais d'un bord ou de l'autre du fleuve.

"A father? Well, he's the one who takes you on his knees when you cry, who sits down beside you in the evening when you're afraid to go to sleep and tells you a story."

The boy didn't answer.

"True, often children haven't had a father," the giant went on, as though reconsidering. "But then, they say, there are sweet young women who light the fire so you can sit down close to it, and who sing you a song. If they go away awhile it's only to cook some food; you can smell the oil heating in the pan."

"I don't remember that either," said the boy in his light, crystal voice. He had drawn closer to the ferryman, who now fell silent; he could hear the man's breathing, slow and even. "I need to cross the river," he said. "I have enough to pay the fare."

The giant bent down and scooped him up in his enormous hands. After setting him on his shoulders, he stood up and climbed down into the boat. It gave way a little under his weight. "All right, let's go," he said. "Hang on tight to my neck!" With one hand he gripped the child by a leg, and with the other he stuck the pole in the water. In a sudden movement, the boy embraced the ferryman's neck, and let out a sigh. Now the giant was able to grasp the pole with both hands; he pulled it out of the mud, and the boat slipped away from the shore. The water rushed more deeply under the glimmering, into the shadows.

A moment later a finger touched his ear. "Listen," said the child, "do you want to be my father?" But he broke off right away, his voice choked by tears.

"Your father! Why, I'm only the ferryman! I never stray far from the riverbank."

« — Mais je resterais avec toi, au bord du fleuve.

— Pour être un père, il faut avoir une maison, ne comprends-tu pas ? Je n'ai pas de maison, je vis dans les joncs de la rive.

— Je resterais si volontiers auprès de toi sur la rive !

— Non, dit le passeur, ce n'est pas possible. Et vois, d'ailleurs ! »

Ce qu'il faut voir, c'est que la barque semble fléchir de plus en plus sous le poids de l'homme et de l'enfant, qui s'accroît à chaque seconde. Le passeur peine à la pousser en avant, l'eau arrive à hauteur du bord, elle le franchit, elle emplit la coque de ses courants, elle atteint le haut de ces grandes jambes qui sentent se dérober tout appui dans les planches courbes. L'esquif ne coule pas, cependant, c'est plutôt comme s'il se dissipait, dans la nuit, et l'homme nage, maintenant, le petit garçon toujours agrippé à son cou. « N'aie pas peur, dit-il, le fleuve n'est pas si large, nous arriverons bientôt.

— Oh, s'il te plaît, sois mon père ! Sois ma maison !

— Il faut oublier tout cela, répond le géant, à voix basse. Il faut oublier ces mots. Il faut oublier les mots. »

Il a repris dans sa main la petite jambe, qui est immense déjà, et de son bras libre il nage dans cet espace sans fin de courants qui s'entrechoquent, d'abîmes qui s'entrouvrent, d'étoiles.

"But I'd stay with you here, along the river."

"To be a father, you have to have a home, don't you understand? I don't have one. I live in the rushes along the bank."

"I'd be so glad to stay near you, along the bank!"

"No," said the ferryman, "it isn't possible. And anyway, look!"

What must be seen is this: the boat seems to sink more and more beneath the man and the child, whose weight keeps increasing by the second. The ferryman labors to push the skiff forward, as water keeps pouring in over the sides. Currents swirl through the hull, reaching the giant's thighs. In his huge legs he senses that the curved planks are giving way. Even so the boat doesn't founder; instead it seems to melt into the night. The man is swimming now, with the little boy still clinging to his neck. "Don't be afraid," he says. "The river isn't that wide. We'll get there soon."

"Oh please, be my father! Be my home!"

"You have to forget all that," the giant answers under his breath. "You have to forget those words. You have to forget all words."

He clasps the small leg—immense already—in his hand again, and with his free arm he swims in the limitless space of clashing currents, of yawning abysses, of stars.

L'ENCORE
AVEUGLE

STILL
BLIND

L'encore aveugle

Still Blind

I

Les théologiens
De cet autre pays estiment
Que Dieu est, mais aveugle.
Qu'il cherche, en tâtonnant
Entre des murs trop proches, c'est le monde,
Le petit corps criant, se débattant,
Aux yeux encore fermés,
Qui lui donnera un regard
Si toutefois il peut
De ses mains maladroites, d'avant le temps,
En soulever les paupières.

L'idée, le rêve de Dieu,
Le rêve de ce fond de la nuit qu'ils nomment Dieu,
Ce serait, simplement,
Me disent-ils,
De devenir cette vie, appelé
Par ce qu'il imagine là, en avant,
Dans un regard. Le rêve, le désir
Qui naît de ces ravins, de ces blocs informes,
De ce bruit, très en profondeur, de source, Dieu,
C'est que ce quelque chose-là remonterait
Par le sang, par le cri, par tout le corps
Vers ce qu'il n'a pas encore,
Un visage, des yeux.

I

The theologians
Of that other country
Deem that God does exist, but is blind.
That he searches, groping
Between the narrow walls we call the world
For a little body crying, floundering
With eyes still closed,
That will allow him to see—
If only,
With his clumsy hands from before time began,
He can open its eyelids.

The idea, the dream of God,
The dream of this chasm of night
They name God,
Would be simply—
So they tell me—to become
This life. He is summoned
By what he imagines: there, up ahead,
In a gaze. The dream, the desire,
Born from these ravines, from these formless blocks,
From this deep-down trickling of a spring
—God—
Is that something might well up
Through the blood, the cry, the whole body
Toward what as yet he does not have:
A face, eyes.

Non, Dieu ne cherche pas
L'adoration, le front courbé, l'esprit
Qui l'invoque, qui le questionne, pas même
Le cri de la révolte. Il cherche, simplement,
À voir, comme l'enfant voit, une pierre,
Un arbre, un fruit,
La treille sous le toit,
L'oiseau qui s'est posé sur la grappe mûre.

Dieu cherche, lui sans yeux,
À voir enfin la lumière.
Il prend, lui l'éternel,
Dans ses mains,
Le criant, le fugace
Puisqu'il n'est de regard que dans ce qui meurt.

Et ainsi recommence-t-il
Dans chaque vie
Et tant qu'elle peut voir, car la ténèbre
Vient tôt, son humble quête
De seulement l'apparence.
Elle est plus que lui, il le sait,
Lui qui est le dedans, lui qui recourbe
La chose sur sa forme, qui l'enténèbre,
Lui qui s'évase
Dans le vol des hirondelles, criantes
Dans le ciel bleu ; et même qui se déchire, qui se dilue

No, God does not seek
Adoration, the bowed forehead, the spirit
That invokes him, that questions him—no, not even
The shout of revolt. He simply seeks
To see, as the child sees: a stone,
A tree, a fruit,
The vine below the roof,
A bird alighting on a cluster of ripe grapes.

God the eyeless
Seeks to see the light, at last.
He the eternal
Cradles in his hands
What is fleeting, what cries out,
Since only what dies has a gaze.

And so in every life,
For as long as it can see—since darkness
Will come to it soon—he begins anew
His humble quest
For mere appearance.
This, as he knows, is beyond him—
He who is the inside, who bends
The thing back on its shape, who turns it dark,
Who fans out
In a flight of swallows, clamoring
In the blue, who even shreds apart, dispersed

Dans la nuée ; mais toujours
Du dedans, de sous la figure, de sous la masse
Qui recouvre la masse, qui recouvre
Les failles et les blocs, à l'infini,
De ce que ces théologiens me disent Dieu.

(Lui qu'on entend
Dans le grincement de la barrière, le soir,
Sous le ciel qui est rouge et s'immobilise
Quand nous rentrons,
Et c'est là du dedans encore, dedans du bruit cette fois,
Et la nuit tombe,
Et qu'on retourne une pierre,
Voyez, me disent-ils,
L'agitation des fourmis hors du monde.)

II

Dieu,
Ce que ces théologiens de là-bas appellent Dieu,
Cherche. Il sait qu'il n'a rien, me disent-ils,
Reconnaître, nommer, bâtir,
Il sait qu'il ne l'imagine pas même, n'y atteint pas.
Espérer,
Il sait que c'est plus que lui. Attendre,
Il sait que c'est plus que lui,

In a cloud—but always
From inside, beneath the face, beneath the mass
That underlies the mass, that underlies
The crevasses and faults, the endless rock
Of what these theologians tell me is God.

(Whom we can hear
At dusk in the creaking of the gate,
Under the red sky that comes to a halt
As we go home:
There it is, from inside again, this time inside a sound.
And if, as night falls,
We upend a stone:
See those ants, they tell me, milling
Outside the world.)

II

God—
What the theologians there call God—
Is searching. He knows
He has nothing, they claim.
To recognize, to name, to build—he knows
These are things he scarcely imagines, much less attains.
To hope:
He knows it is beyond him. To wait:
He knows it is beyond him.

Apercevoir au loin, crier,
Se précipiter les bras ouverts, dans les larmes,
Il sait que c'est plus que lui.

Et parler,
Dire : « Allons, prends,
Regarde, ne pleure plus,
Va jouer »,
Il sait que c'est plus que lui.
Dire : « Bois »,
Se pencher sur l'enfant comme il le voudrait,
Mais autrement,
Avec des mains pour toucher les sanglots,
Avec rien que l'espoir et toute l'alarme,
Il sait que c'est plus que lui.

Dehors, pourtant,
Des voix. Dehors :
« Viens, il est tard,
Rejoins-moi. » Il écoute.
Mais il est ce que l'invisible, ce que la vie
Murent, dans les plus simples des mots.

Il sait qu'il aura beau
Prendre une main,
La main ne sera pas entre les siennes.

Catching sight of someone from afar, crying out,
Rushing forward in tears, with open arms:
He knows it is beyond him.

And even speaking,
Just saying: "Come now, take this.
Look, don't cry anymore.
Go and play":
He knows it is beyond him.
Saying simply: "Drink this"—
Paying attention to the child as he would like,
And yet in a different way—
Touching the sobs of the child with anxious hands,
Overcome by hope and concern:
He knows it is beyond him.

And all the while, outside
He hears voices. Outside:
"Come along now, it's late;
Catch up with me." He listens.
But he is what life, what the invisible
Are walling up
In the simplest of words.

He knows that try as he may
To take a hand,
He will not hold it in his own.

Dieu,
Ce qu'ils appellent Dieu, lui le sans nom,
Cherche. Ils l'entendent qui rôde
Dans le cri de l'oiseau blessé, dans le jappement
De la bête prise.

Et ces théologiens savent donc
Que Dieu s'approche d'eux,
Nuit et jour ; qu'il se glisse dans leurs prunelles
Quand ils ouvrent les yeux. Ils se convainquent
Qu'il veut leurs souvenirs,
Leur joie,
Qu'il veut les dépouiller de même leur mort.

Et toute leur pensée, toute leur vie,
C'est de le repousser, c'est de dire non
Aux mains immenses.
« Éloigne-toi, crient-ils,

Éloigne-toi dans les arbres,
Éloigne-toi dans le souffle du vent qui erre,
Éloigne-toi dans le bleu et dans l'ocre rouge,
Éloigne-toi dans la saveur des fruits,
Éloigne-toi
Dans même l'agneau tremblant du sacrifice. »

God,
The nameless—what they call God—
Keeps searching. They hear him lurk
In the screech of a wounded bird, in the yelp
Of a captured beast.

And so these theologians know
That God steals up on them
Night and day; that as soon as they open their eyes,
He slips inside. They convince themselves
He wants to rob them of their memories,
Their joy,
To strip them even of their death.

The goal of all their thought, all their life,
Is to beat him back—to say no
To his giant hands.
"Go away," they shout,

"Go away in the trees,
Go away in the breath of the wandering wind,
Go away in depths of reddish ochre, and in blue,
Go away in the taste of fruit,
Go away,
Even in the trembling lamb of sacrifice."

Et ils vont sous les arbres,
Ils agitent des banderoles de couleur.
« Allons, éloigne-toi, crient-ils,
Va, désespère,
Allons, lève-toi, pars,
Tu es la bête furtive au cœur maçonné de nuit.

Lâche la main que tu prends,
Elle a peur.

Trébuche, relève-toi,
Cours, enfant nu que l'on accable de pierres. »

And they walk beneath the trees,
Waving colored pennants in the air.
"Hurry up, go away," they shout,
"Go away. Despair.
Now. Get up and leave.
You are the furtive beast whose heart is walled with night.

Let go of the hand you hold:
That hand is afraid.

Stumble, stand up again.
Run. You naked child, pelted by stones."

L'or sans visage

Faceless Gold

I

Et d'autres, d'autres encore. Ceux-ci me disent
Qu'ils savent
Et c'est que Dieu déchire, c'est là le monde,
Les pages qu'il écrit. Que c'est sa haine
De son œuvre, de soi,
De même la beauté dans le ciel des mots,
Qui noircit de sa flamme,
L'arbre de la parole humaine, qui espère.

Dieu est artiste,
Il n'a souci que de l'inaccessible,
Et il a les colères de l'artiste,
Il craint de ne produire que de l'image,
Il crie son impatience dans le tonnerre,
Il insulte ce que pourtant il aime, ne sachant
Prendre un visage entre ses mains qui tremblent.

Et ce que nous devons à Dieu, ajoutent-ils,
C'est de l'aider à détruire, en cessant
De désirer nous aussi, ou d'aimer.
C'est, en nous détournant, en nous taisant,
En recouvrant de cendres la lumière,
De faire que la terre, ce ne soit plus
Que le désordre des roches du fond des combes.
Dieu, ce ne soit

I

And others, still others. They tell me they
Are the ones who know:
God, they say, tears up all the pages he writes,
And that is the world. Like a flame,
His hatred of his work and of himself,
Of even beauty in the firmament of words,
Blackens the tree of human speech,
This hope.

God is an artist
Who cares only for the inaccessible.
He rants with an artist's fits of rage.
He fears he's made an image, nothing more.
He shouts his impatience in thunder.
He insults what he loves:
He's never learned to hold a face
In his trembling hands.

And what we owe God, they add,
Is to help him destroy: we too must renounce
All desire and all love.
We must turn away in silence.
We must smother light with ash,
So earth will be no more
Than jumbled rocks in a ravine.
So God will be no more than blind,

Que l'herbe qui est aveugle aux autres herbes
Sous l'averse qui tombe aveugle. Fassent nos cœurs
Qu'à la place de la parole il n'y ait plus,
Dans les flaques du temps incompréhensible,
Que la boue de cette matière qui rêva Dieu.

L'être : pas même la pierre, prétendent-ils,
Mais la cassure
Qui traverse la pierre, l'effritement
Des arêtes de la cassure, la couleur
Qui n'attend rien, qui ne signifie rien dans la lumière.

II

Mais d'autres me confient
Que celui qu'ils rêvaient avait eu d'abord
Assez d'étonnement pour s'émouvoir
De, par exemple, un enfant
Qui s'était élancé dehors, un matin d'été,
Avec un cri de joie. Plus encore,
D'un qui s'était détourné pour cacher ses larmes.

Dieu désirait entendre, en ce premier rêve,
Ce qu'écoute le musicien, penché
Sur ses cordes vibrantes. Il s'étonnait
Du sculpteur, qui aspire,
Là où le sein se gonfle dans le marbre,

Unknowing grass, under blindly falling rain.
So our hearts will make
The word, in muddy pools
Of incomprehensible time, no more
Than this matter that dreamed God.

Being: less than stone, they contend—
Only a fault
That crosses stone. A weathering
Of ridges in the rift; a color that waits for nothing,
That means nothing in the light.

11

But others have confided
That the one they dreamed
Felt wonder enough, at first,
To be touched when a child
Leapt outside with a cry of joy,
One summer day; and felt moved even more
When a child turned aside, to hide his tears.

In that early dream, God sought to hear
What the musician hears, bending
Over vibrant strings. He was amazed
By the sculptor who aspires
To more than beauty offers him

Où des lèvres s'entrouvrent,
À plus qu'à la beauté qui s'offre à lui.

Et ils m'assurent même qu'une fois,
Regardant s'évertuer un artisan
Sur un morceau de bois, pour y faire naître
L'image de son dieu, dont il voulait
Qu'elle tarît en lui l'angoisse d'être,
Il éprouva pour cette gaucherie
Un sentiment nouveau, il eût désir
De satisfaire ce désir, d'aller vers lui
Dans la matière où trébuchait l'espoir,
Et il s'alourdit, il se fit ce bois, s'incarna
Dans l'image naïve, il se confia
Au rêve de l'artiste.
Dans l'image il attend sa délivrance.

Dieu,
Ce que ceux-là nomment Dieu,
Attend. Il est ce qui végète dans l'image,
Enseveli encore. Et en somme, et pour la première fois,
Ce qui espère. Il entend
Ces bruits qui se rapprochent, qui s'éloignent.
Lourde est sur lui l'humble pensée humaine.
Lourd le poids du regard épris, des mains fiévreuses,
Lourd le dos souple de la jeune fille couchée,
Lourd le feu dans la chambre, qui brûle clair.

In the breast that swells in marble,
The lips that part.

They even assure me that God
Watched a craftsman once, toiling at a piece of wood
To give birth to the image of his god,
So it might quell the anguish being brings;
And as he watched, God felt a newfound awe
Before that awkwardness. They say that he desired
To satisfy desire: he wanted to reach out
To the man through matter,
Where hope was faltering.
He grew heavy, he became the wood;
He made himself incarnate in that naïve shape,
The artist's dream.
Within that image, now he waits
For his deliverance.

God,
What in that country they name God,
Still waits. He vegetates, still buried
In the image; and for the first time, he is
What hopes. He listens
As sounds come near, or trail away.
The humble thoughts of men weigh him down—
Heavy the adoring gaze, the fevered hands,
Heavy the supple back of the girl lying prone,
Heavy the fire in the room, burning clear.

III

Ils me parlent. Quelle étrange chose que leurs voix !
C'est errant au-dessus du sommet des arbres,
C'est rouge et triste comme le son du cor.
Je vais vers là où j'imagine qu'elles s'élèvent,
Je parviens quelquefois à des carrefours,
Deux, trois sentiers couverts de feuilles mortes,
Je m'engage sur l'un, où j'aperçois
Un enfant à genoux, qui joue à prendre
Dans ses mains des cailloux de plusieurs couleurs.
Il m'entend approcher
Et il lève ses yeux vers moi, mais se détourne.

Et quelle étrange chose que certains mots,
C'est sans bouche ni voix, c'est sans visage,
On les rencontre dans le noir, on leur prend la main,
On les guide mais il fait nuit partout sur terre.
C'est comme si les mots étaient un lépreux
Dont on entend de loin tinter la clochette.
Leur manteau est serré sur le corps du monde,
Mais il laisse filtrer de la lumière.

III

They speak to me. How strange their voices are,
Roving above the summits of the trees,
Red and sad as the sound of a horn.
I walk where I imagine they arise,
And at times I reach a crossroads:
Several paths covered with dead leaves.
I enter one of them, and there I see
A child at play on his knees.
He picks up pebbles of different colors.
Hearing me draw near, he lifts
His eyes toward me. But then he looks away.

And certain words, how strange they are:
Without a mouth or voice, without a face.
We come across them in the dark, and take them by the hand.
We guide them, but the night
Is everywhere on earth.
Words are like a leper with a bell
That tinkles in the distance.
Their cloak is pressed
To the body of the world,
But it lets a little light filter through.

JETER
DES PIERRES

THROWING STONES

ROULER PLUS VITE

Pourquoi regardaient-ils l'horizon ? Pourquoi gardaient-ils les yeux constamment fixés sur ce point, là-bas ? Peut-être simplement parce qu'ils roulaient droit vers lui depuis bien longtemps sur cette route nocturne, dont chaque côté n'était qu'une étendue caillouteuse, parfois bosselée de collines basses, avec seulement de rares buissons sous le grand ciel, sans étoiles. Au loin, très loin, deux lignes indéfinies de montagnes. Quelque chose comme deux bras qui, largement ouverts autour d'eux, les appelaient à l'avant, là où semblait se jeter la route. Mais cela faisait tant d'heures maintenant que ce seuil se dérobait, s'effaçait, rejetant loin de l'asphalte nue les pentes imaginées, espérées ! Tant d'heures ! Alors que depuis si longtemps déjà la nuit aurait dû finir.

Ils regardaient l'horizon, le ras du ciel, ils se taisaient, ils ne pouvaient plus détacher leur pensée de ce point où la route perçait la masse noire, indécise.

Et voici qu'une rougeur y parut, soudain, un peu à gauche de l'en-avant de la route, là où tout de même, depuis un moment déjà, le sol se gonflait, à n'en pas douter, se hérissait de bosses et, qui sait, de creux, avec peut-être de l'eau. La rougeur s'accrut, elle élargit sa prise sur l'horizon, des taches de clarté intense, comme d'un feu, s'y firent jour, et le ciel autour d'eux en était déjà presque rose—eux, ils purent se regarder les uns et les autres, dans la voiture, il y avait de ce rose sur leur visage.

Mais la crête enflammée du soleil tardait à paraître. Et au bout de longues minutes la rougeur, qui n'augmentait plus, commença à plutôt décroître puis le fit avec évidence, la flamme qui y bougeait redevenant cendre pourpre, qui s'éteignit. La clarté disparut au ras de ces collines enchevêtrées entre le ciel et le monde. Et ce fut à nouveau la grande nuit d'avant, sans étoiles.

DRIVING FASTER

Why did they keep looking at the horizon? Why did their eyes focus without swerving on that point over there? Perhaps it was just because they'd been driving straight toward it for so long on this road, in the night. On either side was nothing but a stony expanse, studded here and there by low hills with a few sparse bushes under the vast, starless sky. Far away, very far, two blurry lines of mountains summoned them like wide-open arms toward where the road seemed to be rushing. But that threshold had been retreating for so many hours—withdrawing, shoving the imagined, hoped-for slopes away from the naked asphalt for so many hours. For such a long time that by now the night should already have come to an end.

They stared at the horizon, flush with the sky, and never spoke. They could no longer keep their minds off the point where the road pierced that black, indeterminate mass.

Then suddenly a redness appeared a little to the left of the road up ahead, where for quite a while already the ground had been swelling. No doubt about it: humps were buckling up, and there might be depressions too, possibly filled with water. The ruddiness increased, spreading its hold on the horizon. Spots of vivid brightness emerged, as of a fire, and the sky all around was almost pink. In the car they could look at each other now: on each other's faces, they could see that pinkish glow.

But the fiery crest of the sun was slow to appear. At the end of long minutes the redness no longer grew. First it began to pale, then plainly faded. The flame that had flickered turned to crimson ash, and finally died out. Between the sky and the world, at the cusp of these tangled hills, all light had disappeared. And again the great night loomed ahead, empty of stars.

ROULER PLUS LOIN

La route depuis un moment s'était faite elle-même caillouteuse. Puis de la roche avait commencé d'en boursoufler, d'en fendre le sol, ses affleurements ne cessaient plus de s'étendre, de grossir, il fallait que cahotât la voiture sur ces grosses veines qui se déchiraient en des points, répandant par des coulées de gravats rugueux ou de sable une autre sorte de noir, plus épais encore, que celui de la nuit qui régnait désormais sans fin concevable sur le monde. Avancer dans ces conditions, ah, que c'était difficile ! À des moments il fallait descendre du cabriolet—car maintenant la voiture était découverte, on y respirait librement l'air froid—pour le soulever d'un côté et lui permettre ainsi de côtoyer une de ces pierres à peine discernables dans l'ombre, et parfois bien plus larges et longues qu'on n'aurait cru. Et de plus en plus nous avions peur qu'il y eût bientôt au travers de notre chemin une roche encore plus large, qui barrerait le passage. Et qui sait si, alors, nous pourrions nous écarter de la chaussée par une des fondrières du bord pour retrouver plus loin la route qui au-delà allait droit (cela restait vraisemblable) ?

Rouler, pourtant, rouler puisque mystérieusement le moteur ne cessait pas de le consentir, avancer à tout prix, ne pas cesser d'avancer pendant ces grands remuements qui, nous n'osions pas trop le savoir, se faisaient aussi dans le ciel : montagnes, d'eau peut-être, qui s'effondraient, masses vaguement sphériques qui se heurtaient, se repoussaient, se cognaient à nouveau, et bourdonnaient ou tournaient à grands bruits d'abîmes puis se perdaient dans l'incréé, dans l'absence.

DRIVING FARTHER

A little earlier the road itself had started getting rocky. Then the stone began to bulge, splitting the pavement; after that the outcrops thickened and expanded. The car had to jolt along these swollen veins as they broke into sharp points. Night ruled the world from now on, with no conceivable end. Another kind of blackness, even denser, spilled through outflows of sand and rough debris. How hard it was to keep moving in such conditions! Now the car was roofless, and we freely breathed cold air. At times we had to clamber out and lift it to one side to skirt a rock barely visible in the dark, much larger and longer than we'd thought. More and more we were afraid that soon a boulder would lie across our path, blocking our way. Who knew whether then we could branch away from the pavement through one of the gaps along its sides and pick up the road farther on—farther on where it stretched out straight. But was that still likely?

Driving anyway, driving ahead, since mysteriously the engine never gave out. Moving forward at any price, always moving forward. Meanwhile, though we didn't dare to pay them much attention, great upheavals also shook the sky. Mountains, perhaps made of water, would collapse. Vague spherical masses collided, repelled each other and rammed again, humming or roaring as they whirled in the abyss. Then they vanished: into the uncreated, into absence.

JETER DES PIERRES

Et nous étions là, dans la nuit, à jeter des pierres. À les jeter le plus haut, le plus loin possible, dans ce bois devant nous qui si rapidement dévalait la pente que c'en était sous nos pieds comme déjà un ravin, avec le bruit de l'eau à ruisseler en contrebas sous les arbres.

Des pierres, de grosses pierres que nous dégagions des broussailles, difficilement mais en hâte. Des pierres grises, des pierres étincelantes dans le noir.

Nous les élevions à deux mains, au-dessus de nos têtes. Qu'elles étaient lourdes ainsi, plus hautes, plus grandes que tout au monde ! Comme nous les jetterions loin, là-bas, de l'autre côté sans nom, dans le gouffre où il n'y a plus ni haut ni bas ni bruit des eaux ni étoile. Et nous nous regardions en riant dans la clarté de la lune, qui surgissait de partout sous le couvert des nuages.

Mains déchirées bientôt, mains en sang. Mains qui écartaient des racines, fouillaient la terre, se resserraient sur la roche qui résistait à leur prise. Et le sang empourprait aussi nos visages, mais toujours nos yeux se levaient du sol dévasté vers d'autres yeux, et c'était encore ce rire.

THROWING STONES

And we were there in the night, throwing stones. Throwing them as high and far as possible, in woods that plunged before us down a slope so steep it seemed like a ravine. Water was rushing by farther on, below the trees.

We struggled hastily, pulling stones from the undergrowth. Big stones. Gray stones. Stones that glittered in the dark.

With both hands we raised them above our heads. How heavy they were, higher and wider than anything in the world. How far we would throw them now, throw them over there to that other side without a name, that abyss without a high or low, with no roaring waters, no star. And we looked at each other, laughing as moonlight spilled from everywhere, under the cloud-lidded sky.

Hands that were shredded soon. Bloody hands. Hands pushing roots aside, digging at the earth, gripping the rock that strained against our grasp. Blood crimsoned our faces too. But always we raised our eyes from the devastated ground toward other eyes, again with that laugh.

AFTERWORD

by Hoyt Rogers

Water from Stone:
Yves Bonnefoy's *The Curved Planks*

The poetry of Yves Bonnefoy is founded on rock, and inscribed in stone: the primary rock of earth, the weathered stone that bears witness to the dead. Already in his first major essay, "The Tombs of Ravenna," he writes: "I cannot consider stone without acknowledging that it is unfathomable, and this abyss of fullness, this night sheathed by eternal light, for me exemplifies the real." His earliest surviving verse, *The Heart-Space* (*Le cœur-espace*) of 1945—an ephemeral chapbook not republished until 2001—begins with the image of a "face of stone" and goes on to evoke "the flagstones of death" and a "theatre of stone." The mysterious figure that haunts *Of the Motion and Immobility of Douve* (*Du mouvement et de l'immobilité de Douve*), the collection that marks his poetic coming of age in 1953, "raises a gesture like rock in the hard air"; she "shares the hypnosis of stone" and is "as blind as rock." Conversely, rock takes on life when a salamander reveals "stone's first step of consciousness" with its "gaze that is a stone." Published five years later, *Yesterday's Empty Kingdom* (*Hier régnant désert*) alludes to rock's "vast and gray soul," to "boulders of silence," to "stones upon stones, that have built the country said by memory."

The dead beneath their tombstones begin to speak in *Written Stone* (*Pierre écrite*) of 1965; true to the title, Bonnefoy names poem after poem simply "A Stone," a habit he will keep in subsequent works. In all such poems he is referring specifically to the tablets with fading epitaphs that commemorate graves. (The French reader would grasp this readily from the original, because "pierre" standing alone often designates a "pierre tombale," or "tombstone.") But not only do his verses— always center-spaced—reinscribe those half-effaced legends, they also give voice to the dead themselves, whose words often alternate with his own. At the same time, *Written Stone* maintains the rock motif in its primordial sense, as the "exemplification of the real." In its pages, the poet contemplates "a valley of countless stones," "listening to it dream" in a "voice broken at times by an invisible rock"; and dawn arrives as the "radiance of unsealed stones." That last phrase should give us pause. Even in the poems entitled "A Stone," the term figures with greater or lesser ambiguity according to the context, and can often be interpreted as either a gravestone or a rock—or significantly, both at once.

In the Threshold's Lure (*Dans le leurre du seuil*) was published in 1975; though a departure in many ways from the norms of Bonnefoy's verse, it "takes up again the absolute of stones." In the litany of consent at the heart of the work, the poet merges with "the illumined stones of evening," and "stops at the summit of the world among stones." After the open-ended structure of that meditation, *In the Shadow's Light* (*Ce qui fut sans lumière*) of 1987 returns to tauter forms. Scattered through the book are short poems called "A Stone," reminiscent of the lapidary texts of *Written Stone* twelve years before. A disembodied "voice" reminds us that "stone has infinite words"; the stars are described as "thousands of stones in the sky"; even the night is an immense "sparkling boulder that bars the river's course." In *Beginning and End of the Snow* (*Début et fin de la neige*) of 1991, banks of snow tend to hide the rock from view; but it reemerges in memories of summer walks and of the stone architecture in Italy. "Of Wind and Smoke," the only verse sequence in *The Wandering Life* (*La vie errante*) of 1993, a collection consisting mostly of pieces in prose, provocatively compares Helen to a "great reddish boulder" lifted onto the ramparts of Troy, an impervious object of desire. In "A Stone," placed strategically at the center of the volume, the poet yearns to incise a "circle on the rock," some sign of permanent reality; but in the end he is forced to recognize that "the stone closes to our vow."

Bonnefoy further underlines the importance of this brief, talismanic poem by isolating it in a section all its own:

> I still hunger for that place
> That was our mirror, hunger
> For the fruit curved on its waters,
> Hunger for its saving light.
>
> And in memory of how it shone
> I will engrave a circle
> On the rock, an empty fire.
> The sky moves swiftly overhead
>
> As the stone closes to our vow.
> A passion is only a dream,
> Its hands will never ask.
>
> And whoever's loved an image:
> Though his gaze may desire,
> His voice remains broken,
> His words are full of ash.

The bleak resistance of rock contrasts with the life-giving waters that both nourish fruit and reflect it in their "saving light." Often paired, the interlocking themes of water and stone run through all of Bonnefoy's work like an organic axis, a dynamically shifting polarity.

Given the persistence of such metaphors in the author's oeuvre, it will come as no surprise that Bonnefoy's most recent collection of verse, *The Curved Planks* (*Les planches courbes*) of 2001, also abounds in references to stone. In its pages, rain falls on a rocky ravine that is synonymous with "the world," "shadows and stones embrace" in lovers' memories, and a consciousness that might be "God" wells up slowly from the bedrock. In one of the poet's most delicate elaborations of the stone motif, the voices of the dead rise from their tombs:

> Then know an even fainter sound, and let it be
> The endless murmuring of all our shades.
> Their whisper rises from beneath the stones
> To fuse into a single heat with that blind
> Light you are as yet, who can still gaze.

No fewer than nine poems bear the title "A Stone," a higher number than in any of Bonnefoy's books since *Written Stone*, and the volume ends with "Throwing Stones," a brief section of prose poems in which the primary rock of a stony landscape predominates. Though water images come to the fore in this book more emphatically than ever before, they draw their impact from the fundamental leitmotif of rock, the "abyss of fullness" that "exemplifies the real."

The author's thematic continuity may be obvious in retrospect, but it was hardly a foregone conclusion. Decades ago, Bonnefoy used to recount an anecdote that has revealed its deeper meaning in the fullness of time. In 1964, when Jean-Pierre Richard published an essay on the poet's work in his *Eleven Studies of Modern Poetry* (*Onze études sur la poésie moderne*), he identified a cluster of key motifs in Bonnefoy's verse. Apart from stones, Richard listed blood, insects, the salamander, the sword, windowpanes, rivers, forests, and wind. Naturally, it somewhat bemused the poet that his friend seemed to present this catalogue as definitive, when it was based on only his first two major books of verse. After the third appeared, a year later, Bonnefoy greeted Richard with the remark, "You see how much my poetry has changed?" Teasingly, the critic replied, "The more it changes, the more it remains the same."

There was some truth in this, but only a truth the subsequent collections have modulated or undermined. The stones have remained a constant, as have the trees, the rivers, the windowpanes, and the wind. But other elements have virtually disappeared over time, or changed beyond recognition: the spurting blood, the ravenous insects, the salamander, and the sword have all receded from view, just as many other motifs have advanced into the foreground. Bonnefoy was right that his evolution could not be predicted; in fact, few poets have demonstrated such a fertile capacity for self-renewal, or displayed such wide-ranging shifts in theme, image, diction, and form. These transformations are symbolized by the waters that pervade his later poems: snow, rain, rivers—and increasingly, the sea. Melting, misting, streaming, or breaking into waves, water changes the hard contours of a world we can alter only through our own inner vision, our insight. As in the emblematic poem "A Stone" in *The Wandering Life*, water nurtures the fruit of the imagination, the sustenance our hunger needs and sometimes finds. In Bonnefoy's work, stone does not always "close to our vow." Combined with his central sign of permanence, the bedrock that underlies all his verse, water represents the vital metamorphoses of poetry itself—a living spring that flows through all the landscapes of his oeuvre, gathering strength and breadth over time.

Bonnefoy has published seven main collections of verse to date. Loosely speaking, they form a pair of "trilogies" that frame *In the Threshold's Lure*, the central panel of the series. His first great opus, *Of the Motion and Immobility of Douve*, introduces an acute dramatic tension that gradually resolves itself in the following two works, *Yesterday's Empty Kingdom* and *Written Stone*. Ten years separate *Written Stone* from *In the Threshold's Lure*, the most idiosyncratic of Bonnefoy's cycles of poetry. After that pivotal volume, another twelve years elapse before the initiation of the second trilogy, which tonally and thematically links *In the Shadow's Light, Beginning and End of the Snow*, and *The Curved*

Planks. Macabre and febrile, *Douve* still bears traces of the poet's early apprenticeship in the Surrealist movement: the breathless passages that open the work rush forward like a nightmare put into words, and the female figure of the title is dismembered with a ferocity that recalls Lautréamont. But toward the end of the sequence, the violence gives way to the measured austerity that will mark *Yesterday's Empty Kingdom*, in which a stoic resignation overcomes sorrow and denial. Raised to a higher pitch, informed by a newfound love, that acceptance turns to affirmation in the luminous calm of *Written Stone*. As always with Bonnefoy, the epigraphs tell all. A quotation from Hegel places *Douve* squarely under the sign of death, which "the life of the spirit does not fear." *Yesterday's Empty Kingdom* is prefaced by Diotima's two-edged remark to Hyperion, in the novel by Hölderlin: "Because you want a world, you have everything, and you have nothing." By contrast, the heading of *Written Stone* asserts triumphantly, in words from *The Winter's Tale*, "Thou mettest with things dying, I with things new-born." The blood-spattered Douve is transmuted into a lover wearing a red dress, a motif that will recur throughout the poet's later oeuvre. She seems as tranquil as the figurehead of a slow-moving ship, and the wintry rage of the earlier book lapses into a summer of fathomless serenity.

Despite their disparity of tone, the three volumes of this first trilogy are linked by a predominantly dry and rugged landscape. Moisture figures almost as a miracle, like a stream that flows through the desert, or water that issues from stone. Its appearance is greeted with passionate relief, as in these lines from "The Myrtle Tree":

> Sometimes I knew you were the earth. I drank
> The fever from your lips like water welling up
> From sun-struck rocks . . .

Here, as elsewhere in Bonnefoy's work, water is associated with the enlivening gift of love. In "A Voice," the beloved becomes a "flowing spring" that sustains "the leaves" identified with the lover. By inspiring him to embrace life and the quiet passage of time, she also leads him to accept the inevitability of death:

I loved how the wind rose, shouldering the dark,

Loved how even dying in the deep black spring
Would barely stir the pool where the ivy drank.

Similarly, in *The Curved Planks*, a "faraway voice" will teach us to die as softly as a phrase: "Listen, the words fall silent. Their song / Is only sound, and now the sound will end."

As its title implies, *In the Threshold's Lure*—the volume that follows *Written Stone*—hesitates to leave one poetic sphere and enter another. The floating versification of this seven-part poem—Bonnefoy's longest— aptly mirrors its fruitful incertitude. Punctuated by frequent ellipses, the thread of development stops and starts in a way that sets the poem off from Bonnefoy's other work. The epigraph is drawn once again from *The Winter's Tale*, the most significant of Shakespeare's plays for Bonnefoy's poetics; as it announces, *In the Threshold's Lure* wavers between a "world ransom'd" and a "world destroyed." Out of that germinal ambiguity new leitmotifs arise that Jean-Pierre Richard could not have foreseen. The metaphoric boat, a feature of Bonnefoy's verse from early on, now glides into focus more insistently than before; and for the first time it is manned by a "dark oarsman," a clear allusion to Charon. An interrogation about the nature of "God" also weaves its way into the text, even if—in line with the poet's attachment to "negative theology"—he is envisaged as a "God who is not." In other interludes that parallel the author's essays more than they echo his previous verse, he speculates about the essence of poetry. Acting as willful intrusions on these loftier themes, references to television, light bulbs, and a poisoned dog confront the poet's meditations with crude reality. But the most important single aspect of this volume is the redeeming advent of the child, an unprecedented figure in Bonnefoy's work up till then, and one that will strongly distinguish him from most contemporary poets. Though coincident with the birth and earliest years of his daughter, the motif transcends the merely biographical—as always in his oeuvre. The child is accompanied by a complex of other images—luminous gold, trees in flower, and ripening fruit—that will become more and more prevalent in the trilogy to come. In a related innovation, the poem closes with a plea for compassion toward those who, like children, possess "the right of a simple dream":

> He who does not know
> The right of a simple dream, which asks
> To heal the meaning, to calm
> The bloodied face, to color
> Wounded speech with light—
> Such a man, should he be
> Almost a god creating almost an earth,
> Lacks compassion, does not reach
> The true, which is only trust, does not feel
> In his desire clinging to its difference
> The major drift of the cloud.

This concern with the ordinary needs of suffering humanity will be echoed in various sequences of *The Curved Planks*, particularly "In the Lure of Words" and "The House Where I Was Born."

In the Shadow's Light returns to the more concise versification and shorter forms of the poet's first three major books of verse, while expanding the thematic novelties of *In the Threshold's Lure*. Richly laden with the enduring themes as well as the more recent ones, it fuses them in unexpected combinations. From the first page, the familiar boat has grown in size and sprouted a sail; it now has several figureheads at its prow, and leaves the familiar river to brave the sea. Increasingly identified with the poet himself, the archetypal child reemerges now and then throughout the sequence, wandering "at the summit of a tree," "touching the ground with a distracted foot," or continuing his path through the dunes. The "almond tree in the month of flowes" associated with the child multiplies into a stand of trees, and the fruit of the grapevines is "pressed into gold." I suggested earlier that Bonnefoy's major verse cycles can be loosely conceived as two "trilogies" framing *In the Threshold's Lure*; if the first trilogy carves out a rocky domain of dryness and dearth, the second gradually unveils a realm of moisture and fertility. In an overarching metaphor that binds and resumes his entire work, the poet draws water from stone: to quote his ars poetica in *Written Stone*, through the redemptive power of poetry "a desolate voice is washed clean."

From another perspective, *In the Threshold's Lure* is itself the central panel of a triptych, one that celebrates the poet's summer house— Valsaintes, in Upper Provence—and the landscape surrounding it. *Written Stone* expresses the newfound joy of inhabiting the ruined abbey, *In the Threshold's Lure* voices anxiety about maintaining its solitary peace, and *In the Shadow's Light* mourns the final loss of all that the house had meant. At the beginning of the last-named collection, poems such as "The Memory" and "The Farewell" look back on a vanished world with sadness and longing. But by the end of the book, the poet expects the "cluster of what is" to give its wine again to those who thirst. A promise of deliverance informs the epigraph, a phrase from John Donne: "For as well the Pillar of *Cloud* as that of *Fire* . . ." As in the biblical exodus conjured by those words, the years of "homelessness" hold out the hope of dwelling anew in the here and now.

In the Shadow's Light contains three poems that presage the form that rebirth will take—"The Branch," "On Some Branches Full of Snow," and "The Snow"; they focus on a motif virtually absent from Bonnefoy's previous verse. But here again, no one could have foreseen how decisively the poet would adopt this fresh direction. In the following collection, *Beginning and End of the Snow*, the theme becomes multifarious and all-pervasive. The transformation of Bonnefoy's imagery corresponds to novel surroundings—an autumn and winter spent in the woods of New England. Given the ardent complexity of his attachment to the house in Provence, perhaps only a radical shift of landscape could restore his primordial state of wonder, that "second simplicity" he has often invoked in his essays. In her letters, Emily Dickinson calls her poetry "my snow"—white pages that come from nowhere, without warning, and settle in drifts on the table. In his snow poems, Bonnefoy takes up this metaphor and extends it: the snowfall is the emblem of his words, swirling and ephemeral. Written by the wind, these blinding texts obscure the world as much as they interpret it. Their playful markings cover every surface, only to vanish overnight. Paradoxically, before they melt, ice crystals glinting from the trees tease us with glimpses of eternity. A transitory whiteness almost seems to purify the earth; but redemption, like the weather, comes and goes. In the 1883 variant of her poem "Snow," Dickinson captures the snow's basic ambivalence: it "traverses yet halts— / Disperses as it stays." No two poets could be more dissimilar, except in their metaphysical scope; but thematic links naturally arise from their rapt contemplation of the same snowbound landscape. As the crow flies, the Hopkins Forest that gives its name to one of Bonnefoy's poems is less than eighty miles from Amherst. More than any other single factor, his frequent walks in the woods near Williamstown suffused his verse of this period with an unheralded, rejuvenating light. Or to say it the other way round: these poems wend their way through a new geography, an amplified interior.

Against this all-enveloping backdrop, places other than New England still rise to meet us: above all, Italy and the south of France, those consecrated haunts from Bonnefoy's past. Since his youth, Italian art and architecture have strongly shaped his sensibility. In "The Only Rose," the church of San Biagio at Montepulciano reemerges from snow flurries, in the midst of a dream; and moving further back through memory, under the snows of age he rediscovers the Lot Valley meadows of his boyhood. Scattered allusions to Christianity in other poems, such as "The Virgin of Mercy" and "Noli me tangere"—however radical the change in their symbolic charge—serve as distant reminders of a religion that France has largely abandoned. In a similar transmutation, the title story of *The Curved Planks* will refer us back to the ancient legend of St. Christopher. The maturation of Bonnefoy's daughter in "All, Nothing" affords a poignant parallel to remembrances of his own growth and development. Winter scenes in America alternate with visions of summer in Provence and the long-lost abbey. Tellingly, the epigraph to these snow-swept poems is from Petrarch's delightful vignette of Laura beneath a flurry of spring blossoms. On one level this refers to a familiar motif in Bonnefoy's previous work, associating a child with an almond tree in flower. But the Italian verses also affirm the power of love ("qui regna amore") to shatter all our preconceptions, to convert snowflakes into petals, age into youth—and vice versa. Throughout the later poems of Bonnefoy, the seasons are constantly superimposed. Time closes its circle, as winter meditates on infancy; and once connected, the entire ring collapses inward, or opens out on timelessness. Summer leaves recall a snowstorm, and snowflakes swarm like bees.

Of the Motion and Immobility of Douve and *In the Shadow's Light* contain sporadic allusions to rain, but nothing comparable to the sustained imagery of "Summer Rain," the long opening section of *The Curved Planks*. If snow tends to conceal the landscape in *Beginning and End of the Snow*, plunging the world into whimsical abstraction, here the rain caresses its contours with sensuous, shimmering light. From the first words of the cycle, a lucent liquidity bathes every object; a "river of moon / flood[s] the table of earth." The poet gazes at this beauty with all the raptness and reverence of a lover: in the section's title poem, the "cloth of the rain" clings to earth's body, such as "a painter might have dreamed." "Let This World Endure" voices the wish that the "water of an hour's rain" could stream forever "in the light / Along the path." In "Rain Falls on the Ravine" the poet awakens to the "rain of summer mornings"; and as though drifting in a boat he observes

> Boughs entangled like a dream, stones
> With eyes the rapid stream has closed
> And that smile in the sand's embrace.

The coupling of the stark stone imagery so prevalent in Bonnefoy's verse with a rain that consoles, cleanses, and renews seems emblematic of *The Curved Planks* as a whole. But the collection reaches that point by a path far more tortuous and vexed than this serene fusion of metaphors would suggest. Like the boat inscribed in the book's very title, the entire sequence of poems moves forward through the pressure of conflicting elements, sharp oppositions in content and form.

The seven sections of the collection display a tremendous diversity. Perhaps this explains why it is unique among the author's poetic works in not bearing an epigraph: no one phrase could possibly embrace its polymorphous moods. Even more than his other poetry cycles thus far, *The Curved Planks* is linked with Bonnefoy's complete corpus— the essays and tales as well—through crisscrossing themes, tones, and prosodies. To plot them in detail would prolong this afterword beyond due measure, but we can rapidly note some parallels. The nature contemplation, limpid lyricism, and shortened verse forms of "Summer Rain" recall *Written Stone, In the Shadow's Light*, and *Beginning and End of the Snow*. "The Faraway Voice," with its airy lightness and childlike simplicity, again evokes the poems written under the snow's dazzling spell. Not only the title but also the meditative, overarching structure of "In the Lure of Words" refers us back to *In the Threshold's Lure*. "The House Where I Was Born," in which memories from the poet's earliest years meld with reverie and myth, bears comparison to the splendid prose of his spiritual autobiography, *The Hinterland*

(*L'arrière-pays*). The two long poems of "Still Blind" take up themes of "negative theology" and the nature of the sacred, which Bonnefoy often examines in his essays. "The Curved Planks" (which lends its title to the whole collection) and "Throwing Stones" continue the vein of terse parables and lapidary stories previously tapped in such volumes as *Cross Street* (*Rue Traversière*) and *Tales Within Dreams* (*Récits en rêve*). It could well be argued that more than any other single book, *The Curved Planks* exemplifies all the astonishing variety of Bonnefoy's oeuvre.

Though the crosscurrents reach their maximum here, in approaching any of his works we must never forget that each of them consciously enacts a cohesive nexus of ideas; these are not mere adjuncts to his poetic creation, they are its fountainhead. Like Borges, a writer whom he resembles in many respects, Bonnefoy deliberately blurs the traditional boundaries of genre. His essays are densely textured, as laden with visual immediacy as his narratives or verse; in turn, his stories and poems flesh out the ideational contours of his essays. Editor of a voluminous dictionary of world mythology, Bonnefoy has written magisterial studies of Giacometti, Mallarmé, the Roman baroque, Rimbaud, Renaissance art, Shakespeare, and a host of other topics. His poems often weave a close-knit fabric of cultural, historical, and philosophical references. Understandably, many new readers of his poetry may respond initially to its imagery or verbal music more than to its intellectual substance. But on repeated perusal, his poems will gradually disclose a dialogue between concreteness and allusion, embodiment and mind, and apparent contradictions will lead to further counterpoints of speech and thought, inseparable at every stage.

Similarly, the retrospective elements of *The Curved Planks* are not an end in themselves: they serve only to heighten, by contrast, a new departure. As before, in *Written Stone* and *Beginning and End of the Snow*, this transition from the familiar to the unknown is marked by the mapping of a landscape, an unexplored geography. Though the central setting actually remains the same as in the book-length poem

In the Threshold's Lure, its outer edges seem transformed, expanded beyond recognition. While allusions to the lost domain in Provence return now and then, they are usually cast in the past tense of memory, and it is the present of a rain-drenched farm with its barn that predominates. Visible from the house, a ravine gashes the earth. A nearby forest allows for walks along diverging paths, and farther on, two rivers merge before flowing into the sea. Bluffs rise along the coast, and there is a beach where children play; but vineyards and mountains also stretch into the distance. Composite and fluid, superimposed and interlaced, the features of this topography surpass the limits of any given location. They float and recombine in the drifting space of metaphor, the everywhere of dream. Like the ocean where the rivers of these poems converge, these shifting landmarks create a place so vast that it is placeless—though possessed of an undeniable reality. Again and again we encounter images of setting sail, as if the mooring to the abbey of Valsaintes had finally loosened, freeing the poet to rove anew.

In one direction, he undertakes a voyage to the interior, to the remote reaches of his past. "The House Where I Was Born," as its title indicates, vividly revisits some formative moments of Bonnefoy's early years. Often they are refracted through prisms of dream and myth, but at times he presents them with disarming directness. While he has touched on similar recollections in his prose works, particularly in *The Hinterland*, such glimpses of his childhood and adolescence have virtually no precedent in his poetry up till now: this renders them all the more moving. The 2001 republication of his youthful chapbook, *The Heart-Space*, includes an interview in which he speaks of his parents in some detail, and "The House Where I Was Born" recalls them in several forceful passages. Still, it would be a gross mistake to confuse these discreet allusions with the confessional verse so common in English since the sixties, which dissects family traumas with psychoanalytic zeal. As Bonnefoy makes clear in his early book on Rimbaud and in his recent work *Baudelaire: The Temptation to Forget* (*Baudelaire: La tentation de l'oubli*), such influences interest him mainly to the degree they shape a poetic vocation. Integral to that calling is the compassion toward his parents he shows in these poems—or, as he writes in the essay on Baudelaire, "the love that goes to the person as a person, to the absolute of a presence on earth." The fact that "the house where he was born" opens out on other landscapes, on dreams and myths, and ultimately on a humanitarian vision of saving the shipwrecked, amply proves that his true habitation is the house of poetry itself.

In this house without walls, coextensive with the universe, the ubiquitous child of *The Curved Planks* moves with inherent ease. Obliquely related to the poet's daughter in the period of *In the Threshold's Lure*, then gradually becoming identified with the poet's own youth in subsequent works, here the figure emerges as more crucial and polyvalent than ever. Appearing sometimes as a boy, sometimes as a girl, sometimes as a being of indeterminate gender, the child transcends any fixed classification. Archetypal but never abstract, playful but always profound, this recurrent companion may perhaps be understood as an embodiment of poetic awareness, always approaching the world with the freshness of discovery, sensitive to shadow as well as to light. That is why, as in Blake, the child is both knowing and innocent, troubled and illumined, human and divine. "The Paths," among the first poems in the collection, begins with the words: "Paths, O beautiful children / Who would come toward us . . ." Elusive, beckoning, the children are synonymous with byways of the mind that fork and double back in the woods, or that widen suddenly onto a meadow. Internalized, they go along with the poet on his walks, laugh and dance at the fall of night, seek shelter when homeless, ask for comfort when hurt, stretch tall to reach sun-dappled grapes, stroll pensively along the beach, or wade in shallow waves. Again and again children's voices speak to him, talk among themselves, or sing for the sake of song. Whenever they draw near, Bonnefoy's verse becomes light and transparent, too, with shortened forms and simplified rhythms. The childlike "faraway voice" of the sequence by that name is lyric consciousness at its purest and most essential. Appropriately, poem VIII of the series harks back to a venerable model of French poetic grace, the *Sonnets pour Hélène*. As in Ronsard's radiant sonnet (Book II, number XXX), the enigmatic "song" heard by Bonnefoy verges on the wordless clarity of music; dancing like a sylph through space and time, its movements recall Hélène's "divine ballet."

For that very reason, the pristine image of the child partakes of the tragic disjunction that always threatens authenticity in Bonnefoy's work; in the passage from poem VIII just cited, it is Bonnefoy, not Ronsard, who tinges the Renaissance ball with an undertone of "torment." In "The Paths," as in poems III and XII of "The House Where I Was Born," he brings to bear the myth of Ceres, a constant in his oeuvre since *Written Stone*. In his essay on a seventeenth-century painting by Elsheimer, published in *The Red Cloud* (*Le nuage rouge*) of 1977, he explains her significance to his thought as a symbol of the earth—of the finite, the here and now. Like some of his poems, the Elsheimer picture portrays an incident described by Ovid in the *Metamorphoses*. When Ceres receives a drinking cup from an old woman, an impious boy mocks the goddess; to avenge herself, she turns him into a lizard. In his arrogance, he scorns the beauty of the world at his doorstep, and so he forfeits his humanity. By contrast, in poem III of "The House Where I Was Born," the poet emphasizes that the child never meant to scoff at the goddess. At the end of the sequence, it is only by learning to "love Ceres at last, who suffers and seeks" that the child can rejoice in "the simple light that gives us life." But by this point the boy has been conflated with another mythological child: Proserpine, the daughter stolen from Ceres by the god of the dead, and with whom she was finally reunited after a lengthy, arduous quest. In this shifting constellation of emblems—which we should never oversimplify—if Ceres represents earthly plenitude, then the children reflect different stances of the mind toward that basic given: rejection, denial, evasion, acceptance, admiration, or love. On the other hand, Ceres also personifies the human predicament, especially our acute experience of loss, grief, and, more rarely, joyous recovery. As in late antiquity, in all these aspects she manifests a close kinship to Isis, the initiatory goddess conjured by poem V of "The House Where I Was Born."

The obverse of the mother figure in these poems—who assumes many guises besides that of Ceres—is the daunting boatman of the brief tale that lends its name to the entire collection. In "The Curved Planks," a child without parents tries to persuade a ferryman to become his father and give him a home beside the river. In another register, this leads us back to the central theme of "The House Where I Was Born." But here we find the intrinsic homelessness of the child magnified to startling dimensions. Unable to offer him shelter, the boatman is swept away with him on a tempestuous voyage; in the end the curved planks of the skiff give way as it "melt[s] into the night." Like the ferryman, the boy swells to immense proportions, swimming in a "limitless space of clashing currents, of yawning abysses, of stars." Superficially, the boatman resembles the Charon-like ferryman of *In the Threshold's Lure*, as he conveys the child into darkness; but his intentions are good-hearted, and it would be wrong to see him in a sinister light. On another level he might be understood as a non-"God" incapable of saving us, but who, by the same token, sets us free. However, once the boy begins to grow heavier and the boat dissolves away, the analogy being drawn by the poet becomes clear. As Bonnefoy confirmed to me in a recent note, he is deliberately referring to the venerable legend of St. Christopher, who forded a river carrying the Christ Child on his shoulders. "Here as in the legend of St. Christopher," the author commented, "it is the child who is the divine."

Resuming his interrogation of the sacred on another plane, immediately after "The Curved Planks" Bonnefoy places the section "Still Blind," with its two long poems that examine the idea of an insufficient "God." In a sense, this is a new variant of the "negative theology" the poet has often touched upon in his essays over the years: even if "God" exists, he can be apprehended only through what he is not, which effectively removes him from human discourse. In these two poems, the speaker makes a point of distancing himself from "God, / The nameless": "God" signifies only what theologians in an invented country call "God." But paradoxically, that "God" is never far away from us. He wells up from every direction, palpable and inquisitive. He longs to know us from the inside, dreams of seeing through human eyes, fervently desires to become us. In a word, he seeks incarnation. It would be facile here to invoke Christology: in fact, Bonnefoy means just the opposite. Man must not humanize "God," nor must "God" be allowed to divinize man. At the highest level of awareness, the poet may be tempted to "excarnate," to betray his finitude in a flight toward deity. But if he yields to that seduction he will lose the precious gift of death, which alone gives substance and intensity to life on this earth. These poems pose the same problem by turning it inside out: instead of man yearning for godhead, "God" strives to fuse with humanity. In both cases, the delusion must be discarded.

All of Bonnefoy's metaphors are deliberately open-ended; but here again, the figure of the child seems to correspond to poetic consciousness in its elemental form. At the end of the title poem of the section, when the divine approaches men in the guise of a child, they treat him with scorn: angry at his presumption, they pelt him with rocks and drive him away. In the closing passage of the second poem, "Faceless Gold," the speaker encounters another child playing with colored stones, just as the poet plays with language. The child averts his gaze, and in the final lines, words become opaque, "without a . . . voice, without a face." Only in that limited state, without pretensions of god-like revelation, can they "let a little light filter through."

Pursuing the same order of ideas, the three prose poems of the last sequence, "Throwing Stones," could be envisaged as depicting the harsh liberty of man in a universe bereft of all transcendence. On the surface, nothing could be more desolate than the vision of the first two, "Driving Faster" and "Driving Farther," in which a car speeds through a nocturnal moonscape of fractured rock, with no destination in sight.

The initial illusion, in "Driving Faster," that day is dawning finally gives way to the realization, in "Driving Farther," that "night rule[s] the world from now on, with no conceivable end." All the same, even in what may be the bleakest lines Bonnefoy has ever written, a glimmer of hope remains. In "Driving Faster," the deceptive daybreak casts a reddish glow, so that at least the passengers can see each other's faces. More important, while that poem portrays them in the third person, "Driving Farther" employs the first person, as though the writer and the reader were traveling with them, too. Especially in the worst of circumstances, solidarity always seems comforting—the sense that come what may, "we" will all suffer through it together. Revealingly, in the same poem the compensatory gift of freedom is also stressed: "Now the car was roofless, and we freely breathed cold air."

Both these aspects are dramatically amplified in the third poem, "Throwing Stones," in which "we" find ourselves in a wholly different landscape. It is still night, but we are no longer confined to the car. We stand in the middle of woods that tumble down a slope, and we can hear a stream rushing through the deep ravine below. The first poem in the sequence prefigures this moment, suggesting that the hollows in the buckling rock might be filled with water; in another foreshadowing, the mountainous clouds of the second poem, "perhaps made of water, would collapse." Now, in the final poem, the bare rock of the previous two gives way to the vitality that only moisture can bring, embodied here by the trees that grow from the stony earth. As opposed to the lavalike outcrops that block the struggling vehicle in the second poem, these stones are within our reach and under our control. No matter how huge they are, we lift them up together and throw them into the abyss; and though we bloody our hands in the effort, we cannot help but laugh. The moonlight that "spill[s] from everywhere" may be cold, even pitiless, yet it enables us to look into each other's eyes. Like a distant, distorted echo, the imagery recalls "Rain Falls on the Ravine" and its stones "With eyes the rapid stream has closed / And that smile in the sand's embrace."

Throughout Bonnefoy's oeuvre, the unyielding rock of the real is vivified by the living water of poetic awareness, which he identifies with hope. In a seminal essay, "The Act and the Place of Poetry," he writes: "I would like to bring together, I would almost like to identify poetry and hope." In his earlier work, the water of hope is scarce and fleeting. The grave penultimate poem of *Written Stone* begins: "You who are said to drink of this almost absent water, / Remember that it escapes us, speak to us." And another voice answers that despite disillusionment and doubt, the break of day will bring the "radiance of unsealed stones." In abundance, this is precipitation's role in *Beginning and End of the Snow* and the "Summer Rain" sequence of *The Curved Planks*. Ultimately, the melting snows and recurrent rains draw grass and trees from barren rock; they course through fertile valleys in streams that go down to the sea. In both these mannalike avatars, the changes in the landscape wrought by weather are a multifarious emblem for the transmutation of language—and so of our rapport with it and with the world—through the "alchemy" of poetry. The title poem of the section "Summer Rain" holds out that golden promise:

> And soon after, the sky
> Would finally grant us
> That gold the alchemists
> Had so keenly sought.
>
> We would touch its gleam
> On the lower branches,
> And love its taste
> Of water on our lips.

It is significant that such aquatic motifs have steadily proliferated in Bonnefoy's verse over time. Prior to *In the Threshold's Lure*, the symbolic nexus of rock predominates; but each collection since then has progressively multiplied the images of water—springs, basins, jars, puddles, ice, snow, rain, streams, rivers, and estuaries that meet the sea. Only adumbrated in previous works, the ocean finally emerges in *The Curved Planks* as an overwhelming presence. Here more than ever, water is the poet's element—along with its age-old human complement, the boat. The very title of the collection is emblematic of a sea change: for the first time, Bonnefoy gives a nautical heading to one of his books.

The "curved planks" that form the vessel's prow appear at three key points in the work. In the title story they split apart as the giant boatman steers his craft through the swirling currents, but "even so the boat doesn't founder; instead it seems to melt into the night." In poem V of "The House Where I Was Born," the poet dreams:

> I lie in the hollow of a hull,
> Eyes and forehead pressed to the curved planks
> Where I can hear the river knocking.
> Then suddenly the prow rides up. Already,
> I imagine, this must be the river's mouth.
> Even so I wedge my eyes against the wood
> That smells of pitch and glue.
> The images garnered in my sleep
> Have been too vast, too luminous.
> Why look outside again, why see the things
> Words say to me, though unconvincingly.
> I desire a higher or less somber shore.

Here the mention of "images" and "words" implies that like the leitmotif of the child, and like that of the water itself, the boat becomes a metaphor for poetic awareness. By way of metonymy, the curved planks stand for the vessel as a whole; more specifically, they are the part of it that perpetually wedges forward into the floating, often hazardous world that surrounds us. At the end of the first half of "In the Lure of Words"—in terms of lines, the center of the entire collection—Bonnefoy is even more explicit about the meaning of the phrase:

> The planks at the prow of the boat—curved
> So the mind will have a shape to bear the brunt
> Of the unthinkable, of the unknown—are coming loose.
> What do these creaks and splinters tell me now,
> Sundering the thoughts that hope had joined?

The central position of this passage is momentous, since the structure of *The Curved Planks* lucidly inscribes its fundamental emblem. The extremes of water and stone, plenitude and barrenness, shimmering dream and grimmest nightmare, mark respectively the first and final sections, "Summer Rain" and "Throwing Stones." From those antitheses—opposite gunwales of the written "boat"—the collection curves back inward to its "prow": the exploratory voyage "In the Lure of Words," in which the mind presses forward to "take up again . . . its task of light." On one side of that parabola, the "faraway voice" of the mysterious little girl transitions gradually from "Summer Rain"—with its themes of childlike innocence and the benignity of nature—to the sustained meditation on poetry at the midpoint of the volume. On the other side, "The House Where I Was Born" resumes the image of the child on a more troubling note, and the boy's cosmic homelessness in "The Curved Planks" further deepens the disquiet. As for the "God" of the section "Still Blind," he is pathetically incapable of realizing himself in the world; in his impotence, he cannot even soothe an injured child. The cheerless vision of existence in the sequence "Throwing Stones" seems far removed from the peaceful harmony that opens the book in "Summer Rain." Yet these final prose poems are subtly interwoven with redemptive motifs that deflect the reader toward the "prow" again, with its balanced view of man's salvation—or self-deception—through the power of words.

The Curved Planks must be read backward as well as forward to the message at its core. The two longer sections in the first half of the book, "Summer Rain" and "The Faraway Voice," progress with a slowly diminishing calm, while the four shorter sections in the second half, on the other side of the central section, "In the Lure of Words," instill a mounting agitation, stressed by their abrupt verses and swiftly paced prose. Balanced in terms of total lines, the even halves of the poetic "boat" launch a mobile equilibrium; as they strain against each other, they lend each other strength. In major versus minor keys, the varied themes and styles mirror, contradict, and enrich one another in a complex interplay between the axis of the work, its two outer edges, and all the gradations in between. The poems of *The Curved Planks* cannot be fully understood in isolation: their meaning derives from their placement in a parabolic unity, a multidirectional arc. As the title says, they are "curved planks," carefully fitted components within an overriding shape. All the same, the formal integration wrought by the poet hardly implies an esthetic self-containment: porous to the water of life through which it ventures, the hull "creaks" and "splinters"—or even, as in the story of the ferryman, seems to "melt into the night." The probing awareness set in motion by the work continually braves, meets, or merges with the all-encompassing, ever-present ocean, a recurrent metaphor for the world itself.

In the pivotal lines quoted above, from the end of part I of "In the Lure of Words," the master word again is "hope"—as we have seen, a virtual synonym in Bonnefoy's oeuvre for poetry. Let there be no mistake: his is not a poetics of complacency, content with the "lures" of skillful prosody and noble rhetoric. But as "In the Lure of Words" also makes clear, he equally disavows the reverse temptation to "abandon words" for "open-eyed despair." He compares that "chimera" to the seductive snares of Armida's garden, depicted by Tasso in *Jerusalem Delivered*. Rejecting the blandishments of a "beyond," whether Christian, Romantic, or otherwise, he insists that we must face the limits of our finitude, fearlessly and gratefully. At the end of "The Faraway Voice," it is poetry not philosophy that teaches us to die; and for Bonnefoy, that in itself is a form of redemption. Our acceptance of death saves us from "excarnation," from closing our hearts to the here and now of our earth, the "house" into which we were born. This is his daring answer to Hölderlin's question in "Bread and Wine": "What good are poets in times of dearth?" At the heart of *The Curved Planks*, "In the Lure of Words" raises a bold hymn of praise to poetry, and the water it brings to those "who still aspire to drink." Images of stone would seem to have no place in the final invocation, as the ship of poetic truth sails across perilous seas. But the reef skirted by its passengers is a kind of living stone, and their voyage of discovery returns them as before to the terra firma of the real, the changeless bedrock of Bonnefoy's work. Still addressing poetry, he writes:

> Your boat glides on, always dark,
> But with shadows gathering at the prow.
> They sing like settlers of former times,
> When at the end of a lengthy voyage
> Earth waxed larger in the foam,
> And a beacon shone.

> If anything remains
> Besides the wind, the sea, the reef,
> I know that even at night you still will be
> The anchor dropped, the footsteps stumbling in the
> sand,
> The branches stacked, the spark
> Under sodden wood—and then, in the anxious wait
> For a wavering flame,
> The first word that ends the drawn-out silence,
> The first fire kindled in a lifeless world.

TRANSLATOR'S
NOTE

Yves Bonnefoy
and the Art of Translation

In a letter he sent me during the course of this project, Yves Bonnefoy aptly describes the image of the boat as "a fundamental metaphor" of his work. Unfortunately for the translator—to paraphrase Mallarmé—translations are made not with images, but with words. The French word "bateau" corresponds fairly well to the English "boat." Suggesting something smaller than a ship, they both apply to a wide variety of craft, and both have a no-nonsense ring to them. But the word consistently used by Bonnefoy in his verse is "barque," which he calls "one of the most beautiful in the language." In its semantic range, it parallels "bateau"; that is why the English "bark" or "barque" will not do, since the word is far more unusual in our language. Besides, it applies only to a sailing vessel, whereas the boats Bonnefoy brings into play are often propelled by oars or punts. An even thornier problem lies in the subtle realm of tone, of connotation. Though simple and unpretentious, the French "barque" possesses a deep poetic resonance that English approximations cannot match. The feminine gender adds to the term's aural allure, in the literal sense that the indefinite article "une," which so often precedes the word, must end with a mute *e*, like "barque" itself. In French scansion, a mute *e* followed by a consonant becomes softly voiced, like the ghost of an English schwa. To borrow an image from Bonnefoy's tale "The Curved Planks," the *e* before *b* in "une barque" makes a "faint thump," as though the boat were "bumping gently against the dock, or a stone." And the same occurs when the word is followed by a word beginning with a consonant.

Here I am not splitting hairs, as any student of prosody will readily concur. Like every great poet, Bonnefoy is acutely attuned to the delicate music of speech, the way each shading of sound conveys an incontrovertible meaning. The reason the word "barque" is so evocative, he writes, is that "between the consonants the vowel forms the same dark hollow we see in a boat between the curved planks of the prow and the stern." Lacking an identical twin for "barque," I have had to settle for "boat" in the versions published here. Still, in the impossible enterprise of translating verse, at times a windfall can spring from dearth. In this instance, Bonnefoy reminds me that "boat" has accumulated a lyric connotation through such precedents as "the unforgettable lines of Wordsworth from *The Prelude*"; and he cites from Book First:

> One summer evening [. . .] I found
> A little boat tied to a willow tree
> Within a rocky cave, its usual home.

This easy familiarity with English poetry seems characteristic of Yves Bonnefoy, whose knowledge of our literature few can equal. His affinity with our poets is visceral and profound, as one of the most touching passages in *The Curved Planks* attests:

> Then came the day when I first heard
> That extraordinary verse of Keats,
> Evoking Ruth "when, sick for home,
> She stood in tears amid the alien corn."
>
> I did not have to grapple
> With the meaning of these words,

Since it was in me from my childhood.
I only needed to recognize and love
What had returned from the depths of my life.

More than a question of themes, his identification with the masters of
our language extends to the aural textures of their work, as we would
expect from a poet so aware of the tonal nuances in his own. In poem
III of "The Faraway Voice," he expresses his particular devotion to the
iamb, the characteristic foot of English verse:

> Two syllables, a short and then a long:
> The iamb hesitates, but also yearns
> To leap beyond the breath that merely hopes
> And enter into all that meaning gives.

Here, as elsewhere in Bonnefoy's poetry, the prosody of his French ap-
proaches English rhythms with remarkable closeness. Just as Words-
worth's boat dimly haunts the imagery of *The Curved Planks*, the
English iamb threads through its versification like an understated
counterpoint. But the poet's fine ear for our language has furnished
only one of the many strands in his uniquely supple prosody: versatile,
inventive, it wrenches and rends such historic French meters as the
decasyllable and the Alexandrine, yet without wholly abjuring their
fullness of contour. For example, he often employs eleven-syllable pat-
terns to jostle the scansion into asymmetry; and mute *e*'s, which he has
qualified in several essays as "creux," or "hollow," ripple through his
verse like a spectral undertow. At the end of part I of "In the Lure of
Words," Bonnefoy literalizes this undulation through enjambment:
". . . plus rien qu'une / Vague qui se rabat sur le désir" (". . . no more
than a / Wave curling back on desire"). In the original, the crest and
fall are enhanced by the subtle voicing of the mute *e* in "une," a conse-
quence of the scansion rule mentioned earlier. Tellingly, in poem III of
"The Faraway Voice," he also compares the short syllable of the iamb

to a "hollow" ("creux"), rejoining the description in his letter of the "hollow" ("creux") at the heart of the word "barque." As I pointed out in my afterword, the boat is one of Bonnefoy's central metaphors for poetic consciousness, ceaselessly embarking on its voyage of outer and inner exploration. When I translated that verse, he asked me to give "creux" an uncommon inflection, rendering it as "depths"; clearly, in both uses of the term, he is positing a generative void, an absence in which presence may be born—or a dynamic, inward space where they cohabit and intersect.

Unlike Borges, whose grandmother was British, Bonnefoy did not absorb the "second music" of a foreign tongue from his family. Building on the instinctive rapport he felt for those lines of Keats, he has developed his affinity with our language through many decades of recasting English verse into French. In fact it could easily be argued that he is not only the greatest living poet, but also the greatest living translator in France. Thus far he has produced brilliant renderings of no fewer than eleven of Shakespeare's plays, as well as a large number of his sonnets and longer poems. He has also received acclaim for his accomplished versions of Donne and—not surprisingly—Keats. Throughout this large corpus of translations he displays an uncanny ability to echo the iambic beats of the originals, despite the natural recalcitrance of French to marked accentuation. As I noted earlier, this extensive praxis has undoubtedly affected the prosody of his own poetic work. His knack for transposing images from one language to another is equally impressive, given the traditional tendency of French lyric vocabulary toward a higher degree of abstractness than our English lexicon (a convention overthrown in the last century by such diverse poets as Saint-John Perse and Francis Ponge, with their densely varied, keenly targeted choice of words).

Bonnefoy's eminence in the translating field was further confirmed in 1989 by the publication of the bilingual *Forty-five Poems of Yeats* (*Quarante-cinq poèmes de Yeats*), a series he had been accumulating for many years. To my mind, this is the most intelligent selection of Yeats's verse ever made, well worth owning even for those who have no French. But for those who do, it is nothing short of a revelation. It epitomizes that "re-creative" process Bonnefoy propounded early on in his essay "The Translation of Poetry," later republished in *Conversations on Poetry* (*Entretiens sur la poésie*). Given his eloquence on the subject, any comments of my own would seem superfluous, and so I prefer to summarize his remarks here.

He begins by asking a basic question: "Can we translate a poem?" In a literal sense, he concludes, we cannot. The original relies on all the givens of its language, and these must largely be jettisoned. "But that is all the better," he suggests, "since a poem is less than poetry: doing without it spurs us on." Instead of replicating the work, we should try to go back to its source. As he explains in the key passage of the essay:

> We should relive the act that produces the poem—the very act that also founders there. Its frozen form is but a trace of the poet's first intention, his primal intuition (call it a longing, an inkling, something universal). By releasing that impulse, we may be able to renew it in another language, all the more authentically because the poet's own dilemma will arise again for us. The language of our translation, like that of the original, will paralyze the questioning that is our speech. Here is the conundrum we face: while language is a *system*, the speech of poetry is *presence*. Yet by grasping that fact we can draw closer to the author, perceiving more clearly the tyrannies he must endure, the mental strategies by which he counters them—and also the fidelities he needs. Unavoidably, words will try to lure us into their own way of being. Starting out as the helpmates of a good translation, soon they champion the bad poem our translation has become. They cripple the experience through bondage to a text. We have to proceed with caution: the ontological rightness of our newfound images matters much more than whether they match term by term, in a skin-deep resemblance, those of the

original. It is an onerous task, but in return we are assisted by the author we translate—if he is Yeats, if he is Shakespeare or Donne. Instead of sitting as before over a mass of text, we revisit its source, where possibilities bourgeoned. We set out on a second crossing, this time with the right to be ourselves.

Though Bonnefoy wrote these words in 1976, before he had composed the majority of his translations, they are already distillations of a past and future master of the art.

All the same, the translator's craft is best revealed by specific examples rather than general principles; he gives several in his essay, one of which I will quote further on. But first, a personal recollection, from an English-speaker's point of view, may help to illustrate how deftly Bonnefoy puts his precepts into practice. In August of 1987, I spent a week with him in Sligo; that summer he had been invited to lecture at the International School, while completing his translations of Yeats. The afternoon of our arrival, he read me his version of that perennial favorite "The Lake Isle of Innisfree," to try it out on a native Anglophone. I must confess my skepticism that anyone, even he, could render this magical incantation—fraught with Old English words—into a Romance language. But as soon as I heard his solution to the fourth line, I was not only convinced, I was moved. "And live alone in the bee-loud glade": that second phrase, peculiar and vivid, seems truly untranslatable. To my surprise, Bonnefoy had mysteriously transposed its strange cadence into French: "Et dans ma clairière je vivrai seul, devenu le bruit des abeilles." (Literally: "And in my clearing I will live alone, become the sound of bees.") Those final words capture not only the music (based on sprung rhythm and impure internal rhyme), but also what is far more difficult, the striking oddness of the original. The ingenious twist by which the lyric self has "become the sound of bees" discards the obvious sense in favor of a vital renovation. The superficial meaning of the line is somewhat altered, but its poetic rightness resounds anew from "the deep heart's core."

To cite another instance of his skill, as it was brought home to me that memorable day in Ireland, I must mention his crucial choice of the verb "vaincre" ("vanquish") to render "break" at the end of "Byzantium"—"the *other* Byzantium poem," as we wryly called it. Bonnefoy was concerned at the time that he might have departed too drastically from the semantic content of the text. But as I assured him, this substitution not only saves the fierce percussion of the original, it also clarifies—though not too much—its convoluted syntax. Ideally, transference to another tongue should enrich, not impoverish a work. In his translations from the English, Bonnefoy accomplishes such feats of discernment again and again, so that many of them rival the originals. His versions of Shakespeare, Donne, Keats, and Yeats not only enhance our understanding of those poets, but they are also splendid poems in their own right, signal additions to French literature.

As such they form an integral part of Bonnefoy's creative achievement. In the bibliographies at the end of his books, he always makes a point of listing his translations along with his other titles. Another passage of the essay quoted earlier states the credo behind that gesture:

> In a practical sense, if translation is not just a copy and a technique, but a questioning and an experience, it can only be inscribed—only be written—in the duration of a life, and by invoking all the acts and aspects of that life. This does not mean that the translator has to be a "poet" in his or her own right. But it undoubtedly implies that if he does write himself, he will be unable to divide his translations from his works.

He goes on to recount that in translating Yeats's poem "The Sorrow of Love," he rendered "labouring ships" as "vaisseaux qui boitent / Au loin" (literally: "vessels that limp / Afar"). In his opinion, that solution failed to retrieve the ambiguities of the original, and yet it imposed itself on his mind with a queer insistency. Eventually, the phrase would resonate in his own poetry. First he wrote some verses directly inspired by the metaphor, but soon he felt compelled to destroy them "so [his] translation could live": it would be hard to imagine a greater tribute to the validity of the craft. The fruitful symbiosis between translation and creation did not end there. Directly or indirectly, *In the Threshold's Lure* and many of Bonnefoy's subsequent poems refer to Ulysses' ships leaving Troy and to his divagations on the way to Ithaca. The defeated city represents both a scene of destruction and a point of departure. To take an example from *The Curved Planks*, its pivotal poem "In the Lure of Words" begins with an extensive allusion to Ulysses and closes with a related metaphor: a perilous voyage of discovery that is also a journey home. In *The Wandering Life*—a title that speaks for itself—"Of Wind and Smoke" develops the Trojan motif at length, only to culminate in a terse and somber envoi:

> These pages are translations. From a tongue
> That haunts the memory I have become.
> Its phrases falter, like what we recollect
> From early childhood, long ago.
> I built the text again, word for word:
> But mine is only shadow. Now we know
> All origin is a Troy that burns,
> All beauty but regret, and all our work
> Runs like water through our hands.

The full stop in the first line mimics the French: Bonnefoy's punctuation emphatically identifies translation with creative work, even though in this haunting coda both partake of a tragic hollowness. Whatever the context, when a poet of his stature calls his own verses "translations," he confers a high accolade on the translator's art.

Taking the process one step further, I can affirm that my familiarity with Bonnefoy's renditions into French has helped me translate his work into English. For example, the freedom with which he reshapes Shakespeare's sonnets into poems of up to twenty verses has encouraged me to rearrange the lines of some of Bonnefoy's strophes, particularly the longer ones. On a more elusive plane, in many of his versions of Yeats he adopts a distinctly Baudelairean tone: I am thinking especially of his brooding and magnificent rendering of "Her Vision in the Wood" and, in a different strain, his poignant recasting of "The Wild Swans at Coole." Given Bonnefoy's avowed closeness to Yeats, I have done my best to tilt some of my translations toward the Irish poet's style—above all when Bonnefoy's Yeatsian rhythms and motifs make that slant almost unavoidable. In passages where he meditates on "beauty and truth" or employs the simple diction linked with the archetypal child, Keats becomes the natural paradigm for the English version, just as he seems to have been for the French. At other junctures, the theme of the child elicits echoes of William Blake.

Bonnefoy's affinity with these authors doesn't make our task any easier; after all, his own voice predominates throughout, unmistakably. No translator should nurse facile self-delusions about "transposing the French back into an English original." Obviously, the ambitious goal of translating one great poet and imitating another at the same time is doomed to failure—the most we can hope for is a modest coloring, a hint of what might have been. But as Bonnefoy remarks in the essay on translation quoted earlier, all poetry falls short of putting its deepest impulses fully into words: there again, the translator's experience must reenact that of the author. Needless to say, in stirring up poetic crosscurrents of this kind, the translator is also declaring his or her own allegiances. As the repeated Baudelairean note in Bonnefoy's versions proves, translators retain their loyalties within their literatures as well as outside them.

A final illustration may serve to clarify what I mean. Earlier I mentioned "The Only Rose," the culminating poem of *Beginning and End of the Snow*, in which the poet dreams of a city "where he might have spent another childhood," composed of buildings as beautiful as those of Alberti, San Gallo, Palladio, or other Italian architects who have inspired him since his youth. At the crux of these verses we find ourselves before San Biagio, an edifice emblematic of the Renaissance. Yet the snowfall Bonnefoy conjures there is purely imaginary, as strongly sensed inside the church as outside it. When he enters the portal, the wintry evocation fuses with a memory of summer, a meadow full of bees where he played as a boy. Just as the boundary between exterior and interior is effaced, now the past merges with the present of dream, so that time hovers suspended:

> I move forward under the archway of a door.
> Snowflakes whirl, blurring the line
> Between the outside and the inside of this room
> Where lamps are lit—themselves
> A kind of snow, flickering
> High or low amid this night:
> As though I had reached another threshold.

> And beyond it is that same humming of bees
> In the sound of the snow. What they said,
> The unnumbered bees of summer, seems
> Reflected by the lamps, and without end.

> And how I would love
> To run, as in the bee-loud days, kicking
> The pliant ball, for it may be
> That I am sleeping now, and dreaming, and following
> Those childhood paths.

Despite the obvious differences of context and versification, these lines have always reminded me of "The Lake Isle of Innisfree." As in that poem, the triple reference here to the bees and their humming— twice mentioned in Yeats—endows the passage with a distinct auditory background, that "sound not yet music" that Bonnefoy has identified with poetry itself. But the similarity goes deeper than a shared metaphor. Like "The Only Rose," Yeats's poem collapses all tenses into one: what begins as a future intention reveals itself as a present rooted in the past. In the central strophe, the poet knows that "peace comes dropping slow" on Innisfree, because he has already experienced it; and by the final stanza, he hears the island's sounds "night and day," in the timeless tense of the "deep heart's core." Like Bonnefoy's oneiric church where snowflakes fall, reminiscent of summer bees, the "bee-loud glade" where the poet lingers even "on the roadway, or on the pavements grey," occupies the placeless place of poetry. Stored like honey, the crystallizing poem "drops slowly" into plenitude, as the visual rhyme of "hive" and "live" affirms: its words coalesce in that dense inwardness where dream and reality are one.

Rightly or wrongly, when I translated "The Only Rose" I decided to highlight the link I perceived between these poems, by deliberately echoing the auditive nostalgia of "Innisfree." While I would argue that my wording still conveys the fundamental sense, I also aimed to pay tribute to Bonnefoy's versions of Yeats, and to the ties his work has spun between our literary traditions. In French the key phrase toward the end of the passage reads "au temps de l'abeille"—literally, "in the time of the bee." As I pointed out earlier, Bonnefoy transposes the "bee-loud glade" of "Innisfree" into "devenu le bruit des abeilles," modifying the exact semantic charge with a related metaphor. Following his cue, in my recasting of "The Only Rose" I render his own phrase there as "the bee-loud days," memorializing his daring modulation of Yeats and the original from which it sprang. By so doing, I hoped to mirror the triple metaphor that hovers in Bonnefoy's poem among the bees, the lamps, and the snow. Etymologically, the Greek equivalent of "translation" is "metaphor": both words mean transference, the displacement of meaning from one context to another. The translated poem can be understood as an extended metaphor that shifts the terms of the original into a different linguistic field. A time-honored theory asserts that poetry is essentially the art of metaphor—of image to image, word to word, sound to sound; and if that holds true, then translation participates in its prime creative act.

But this is not Bonnefoy's view of poetry, as his essays cogently attest. He insists on the poem's capacity to "transgress" metaphor, to defy the figures of rhetoric. Paradoxically, we must marvel at his mastery of the inherited devices, even as he subverts and baffles them. In one of his most compelling early poems, "La Beauté," he envisions Beauty as racked on the wheel and trampled in the mud; and in "The Only Rose," it is mud on the flagstones that ultimately limns the rose of the title. Yet without the beautiful, without the portal opened by the Renaissance façade—also described as "traced like a flower"—the poet's renewed awareness of the real would lose its strength. This dialectic between the deceptive transcendence of the ideal and the redeeming truth of the finite, the here and now, forms the crucible where compassion begins to gleam. Despite his dazzling meditations on art, Bonnefoy is the opposite of an aesthete. In "Faceless Gold," he portrays the sculptor as demanding more than a perfect shape can give; similarly, the willful countercurrents of his verse—the jumps in meaning, the eddying allusions, the prosodic variance, the stylistic twists from poem to poem, even at times from line to line—thwart any tempting lapse into easy eloquence, precisely when its "lures" might seduce us most. In a sense, the imaginative leaps Bonnefoy sometimes makes in his translations parallel the "transgressions" in his own verse, so that once again, the rupture with facile routine allows us to relive the poetic breakthrough at its source.

As for my own versions of Bonnefoy, I must humbly despair of returning him the compliment he has paid to our native tongue. But at least I have tried to apply his methods, seeking the inner rather than the outer significance of his words, bending the imagery when English diction demanded it, and in general, upholding the spirit over the letter. At the same time, I have conscientiously observed the "fidelities" he mentions in his essay on translation. Readers of *The Curved Planks* must judge whether I have taken too many liberties, or too few. Of necessity, stubborn conundrums still linger, reminding us that the European languages closest to our own are in fact "false cognates" writ large. Punctuation affords the most visually striking example. Commas, profuse in French, must often be altered into semicolons, colons, dashes, or periods in English. While current literary French still employs exclamation marks in serious contexts, in literary English they are now relegated largely to the realm of satire or pseudo-naïveté. To transport them wholesale from Bonnefoy's text into the English would skew his intentions entirely, and so I have usually replaced them with other markers, or omitted them altogether.

On a semantic level, one of the knottiest problems was posed by the crucial, recurrent expression "la maison natale." As the author rightly pointed out to me, the term could never be rendered as "childhood home," the phrase that most naturally comes to mind; and yet paraphrases such as "house of birth" or "house of my birth" sound vague and artificial. In the end I have settled for a coinage advanced by the poet, "the house where I was born," despite my concern that it may fall short of the broader implications of the French. At least this expression has the virtue of specificity, in line with our current bias in English verse toward concreteness (not necessarily a constant of our poetry, as Sidney, Vaughn, Pope, Shelley, Tennyson, late T. S. Eliot, and many of Shakespeare's sonnets might prove). Finding an English dyad for "bruit" and "son" in "The Faraway Voice," without having recourse to "noise," was just as arduous; in that quest Bonnefoy's wife, the American artist Lucy Vines, ingeniously rose to the occasion. Finally, with "la parole," I ran up against the greatest challenge of all. English does not possess any ready lexical distinction between the term "mot" and the weightier expression "parole." In addition, for Bonnefoy the word is fraught with a philosophical meaning that goes beyond the most solemn consecrations elsewhere in French literature: it lies at the heart of his work, like a crossroads where all paths eventually lead. At the author's request, I have avoided relying too heavily on such well-worn approximations as "speech" or "words"; instead I have varied the solutions, sometimes in a way that may seem unorthodox. In these and myriad instances of lesser moment, too many to recount, another translator might have hit on different stopgaps, bartering another set of feints for the unattainable truth.

In a translation as in any work, the transposing writer's own identity will intervene with far greater insistence than might be expected, no matter how neutral he or she strives to be. This is not merely normal, it is salutary. As Bonnefoy observes in his introduction to the Yeats volume:

> In translating these poems I have been obliged to go over my thoughts again, to revive dormant intuitions, to meditate on poetry as a whole, to tighten the strings of my own instrument. Here again, my experiences, my memories, my longings, have been invested more than ever in my reading of someone else. And my translations have been impinged upon as well by my blindness, my impatience or my ignorance: that is pernicious, of course, but it does tend to restore a certain consistency to the words, the layered grain of authentic poetry. Here we may point to an advantage, alongside the undeniable dangers. The more a translation interprets a poem by making it explicit, the more it reflects the translator, with all his or her differences from the author. But to be truly faithful, we have to be free. And do we have any freedom if we are not entitled, every now and then, to leap ahead of ourselves as we read? To translate does not mean to repeat: it means to be won over; and that only happens when we put our own thoughts to the test as we proceed.

No matter how monumental the artistic stature of our masters, as readers we have a direct, almost familial access to them through their work. Translation is the closest form of reading, and Bonnefoy once commented that we should "translate our next of kin," the authors to whom we feel most intimately linked. Thanks to a fortunate circumstance, that reading and translating communion has been immeasurably enriched by face-to-face exchanges with Yves Bonnefoy that began in 1969, when I made my first translations of his poetry. At nineteen I had the extraordinary privilege of visiting his study in Montmartre every week for a so-called tutorial—in fact, an unforgettable series of lengthy conversations—and my filial esteem for him has only increased over time. Whatever their defects, these English versions of his verse honor nearly four decades of a chosen "next-of-kinship," one that continues to guide my steps in countless ways.

BIBLIOGRAPHY

Translations of Bonnefoy
into English

All the translations in the preceding pages are my own, except for the English versions of several book titles (see below). For a recent bibliography of the author's works in French, as well as a useful compilation of secondary sources in both languages, the reader should consult one of the volumes listed here: *Shakespeare and the French Poet*, edited by John Naughton. With more dedication than any other single scholar, Naughton has introduced Bonnefoy's vast and varied oeuvre to the English-speaking world.

The Act and the Place of Poetry: Selected Essays. Edited by John Naughton. Translated by John Naughton and others. Chicago: University of Chicago Press, 1989.

Derniers raisins de Zeuxis / The Last Grapes of Zeuxis. Translated by Richard Stamelman. Montauk, N.Y.: Monument Press, 1993.

Early Poems, 1947–1959. Translated by Richard Pevear and Galway Kinnell. Athens: Ohio University Press, 1993.

Encore les raisins de Zeuxis / Once More the Grapes of Zeuxis. Translated by Richard Stamelman. Montauk, N.Y.: Monument Press, 1990.

L'horizon / The Horizon. Translated by Michael Bishop. Halifax, N.S.: Editions VVV Editions, 2003.

In the Lure of Language. Translated by Michael Bishop. Halifax, N.S.: Editions VVV Editions, 2003.

In the Lure of the Threshold (Dans le leurre du seuil). Translated by John Naughton, in *Temenos 6,* 1985.

In the Shadow's Light (Ce qui fut sans lumière). Translated by John Naughton, with an interview with Bonnefoy. Chicago: University of Chicago Press, 1991.

In the Threshold's Lure (Dans le leurre du seuil). Translated by Yves Bonnefoy. Montauk, N.Y.: Monument Press, 2001.

The Lure and the Truth of Painting: Selected Essays on Art. Edited by Richard Stamelman. Translated by Richard Stamelman and others. Chicago: University of Chicago Press, 1995.

The Lure of the Threshold (Dans le leurre du seuil). Translated by Richard Pevear. In *Poems, 1959–1975.* New York: Random House, 1985.

Mythologies. Edited by Yves Bonnefoy. Translated by Wendy Doniger. Chicago: University of Chicago Press, 1991.

New and Selected Poems. Edited by John Naughton and Anthony Rudolf. Translated by Galway Kinnell and others. Chicago: University of Chicago Press, 1995.

On the Motion and Immobility of Douve (Du mouvement et de l'immobilité de Douve). Translated by Galway Kinnell. Athens: Ohio University Press, 1968; Newcastle upon Tyne: Bloodaxe Books, 1992; also in *Early Poems, 1947–1959.*

The Origin of Language and Other Poems. Translated by Susanna Lang. Montauk, N.Y.: Monument Press, 1979.

Poems, 1959–1975. Translated by Richard Pevear. New York: Random House, 1985.

The Primacy of Gaze: Some Remarks About Raymond Masson / La primauté du regard: Quelques regards sur Raymond Masson. Translated by Anthony Rudolf. Birmingham, Eng.: Delos Press, 2000.

Les Raisins de Zeuxis et d'autres fables / The Grapes of Zeuxis and Other Fables. Translated by Richard Stamelman. Montauk, N.Y.: Monument Press, 1987.

Selected Poems. Translated by Anthony Rudolf. New York: Jonathan Cape/ Grossman, 1969.

Shakespeare and the French Poet. Edited by John Naughton. Translated by John Naughton and others, with an interview with Bonnefoy. Chicago: University of Chicago Press, 2004.

Things Dying, Things Newborn: Selected Poems. Translated by Anthony Rudolf. London: The Menard Press, 1985.

Traité du pianiste. Translated by Anthony Rudolf. Birmingham, Eng.: Delos Press, 1994.

Transmorphosis. Translated by Richard Stamelman. Montauk, N.Y.: Monument Press, 1997.

Words in Stone (Pierre écrite). Translated by Susanna Lang. Amherst: University of Massachusetts Press, 1976.

Written Stone (Pierre écrite). Translated by Richard Pevear. In *Poems, 1959–1975.*

Yesterday's Empty Kingdom (Hier régnant désert). Translated by Richard Pevear. In *Poems, 1959–1975.*

Yesterday's Wilderness Kingdom (Hier régnant désert). Translated by Anthony Rudolf. London: MPT Books, 2000.

9 780374 530754